Finding the Grace to Grieve

Finding the Grace to Grieve

Stephanie Jahnke

Carpenter's Son Publishing

Finding the Grace to Grieve

Published by Carpenter's Son Publishing, Franklin, Tennessee
Carpenterssonpublishing.com

Cover and Interior Design by Suzanne Lawing

Printed in the United States of America

ISBN: 978-1-956370-43-0 (print)

Dedicated To

My love, John

My kids, Sarah, Micah, and Joshua—
I am honored that God has entrusted you to me

My sweet Alanna Grace, I can't wait to hug
you when I get to heaven, too

Acknowledgments

Majetta Morris, editor and coach at bright.light.editing.coach@gmail.com. I am so thankful for your help and support over the past three years. You have encouraged me, prayed for me and have become a treasured friend. Your wisdom helping me put this story into words has been such a valuable gift. You have so beautifully transformed my jumbled mess of thoughts into the finished work it is today.

Shane Crabtree and Clovercroft Publishing Group, your wisdom and expertise has made it possible to bring this project to completion. Every bit of advice and instruction has been extremely beneficial and I'm thankful for all your work in accomplishing this great task.

John, I could not have completed this without your constant encouragement. So many days of tears and feeling like I'm not good enough or educated enough to do this were met with your love, a smile, a hug, and the reassurance to keep going. Your unwavering faith in our Heavenly Father inspires me every day to want to know

Him more. There is no one else I would have wanted to take this journey of life with than you.

David & Brenda Perkins (my parents) and **Mark & Nancy Jahnke** (John's parents), You shared in every joy, every heartache, every memory. You walked with us, prayed for us and our babies, helped me remember details, and nudged me along through the difficulty of writing this story. Thank you for loving us and raising us to know Jesus. I know you look forward to hugging your granddaughter as much as we do.

To my Heavenly Father, You have given me an impossible task that I never could have accomplished on my own. It was only by Your unending grace and favor that I even have a story to write. I want to honor You in all I do.

Foreword

"I think I need to go to the doctor. Something's wrong," Stephanie said with a grimace of pain.

"Okay. Call them, and let's get an appointment," I replied.

Stephanie was able to convince the nurse to let us come in for an evaluation, and we walked into the doctor's office fully confident that everything was going to be fine with hopes of being home in an hour or two. After just a couple of minutes in the exam room, the doctor said, "We need to get over to labor and delivery. You are dilated to a 5."

Wait...What?! I thought, *We still have fifteen more weeks until our girls are supposed to be delivered!* Stephanie and I looked at one another in shock. What was going on? It seemed like everything had been going perfectly with this pregnancy. Both of our girls were developing beautifully, the monthly ultrasounds were so much fun as we observed their growth, and Stephanie's health was good. After persevering through infertility for a couple of years, we were excited about having twins, feeling like we were making up for lost time. However, this was the start of the most challenging days we had faced together. Up until that point, we had seen the blessings of God in our lives many times, and most things seemed to have just come naturally. Sure, we had experienced struggles, but nothing that was not typical in life or beyond what we could handle. On the contrary, this would be something far beyond our control and much more difficult than anything we had faced. Furthermore, our time in the hospital with our daughters was filled with more bad news than we had ever heard in our lifetime.

Because of the tremendous heartache experienced during that time, I knew writing this book was going to be an arduous task for Stephanie, and I am so proud of her for striving to produce a work that will be a blessing to so many and honoring to God. Continuously praying that she would be led by the Holy Spirit in everything she wrote, she poured her heart into every word. Countless times stopping to weep, Stephanie pressed on in obedience to what God had called her to do—share her story. Even as she relived and recorded her journey through grief, the Lord completed a healing in her that produced a greater understanding and deeper comfort, just as He will do for you as well.

You see, everyone's story matters. Even though we all have different complexities in our experiences, we are able to comfort one another with the same comfort we have received from the Lord. All of us deal with loss, and this book is so needed to help each of us navigate our own journey through brokenness, grief, and healing. Furthermore, Stephanie's unique perspective as a pastor's wife will be a great resource to other women in ministry who feel they must have it all together. Like Stephanie, you might be feeling alone in your struggle, laboring to put on a smile, pretending to be okay, all while trying to get through the turmoil inside. May you find the courage, through reading Stephanie's story, to reach out to God and others for the support you need. It is okay to not have it all together. It is okay to go through the mourning process, in fact it is absolutely necessary.

As you read through each chapter, I pray that the principles Stephanie came to understand and the comfort that she found will be a great help to you, whether you are grieving the loss of a child, a spouse, a loved one, or a friend. Having personally witnessed Stephanie listen to and comfort several individuals dealing with grief, I know that will be the case. I am confident that as you read Stephanie's journey, you too will find the grace to grieve.

~John Jahnke

Contents

Prologue

On the morning of my fortieth birthday, my husband, John, and our three kids decorated the house, spoiled me with gifts, and cooked my favorite breakfast—jalapeno popper eggs. John then took the kids to pick out flowers. While they were out shopping, I drove to a local coffee shop for my usual white chocolate caramel latte and decided to go for a walk. I remember the day so clearly. It was warm enough to not need a jacket, yet cool enough that I could enjoy my warm cup of deliciousness. The sun was shining brightly, and it was a beautiful day. As I reflected on how tremendously blessed my life was, I began talking to God about it all. I thanked Him for my family, my amazing husband, and children. I thanked Him for the beautiful sunshine I knew was a gift from Him just for me that day. I thanked Him for the life He had given us. The walking path around our neighborhood is about a mile long, and I cherished every moment as I talked with my Heavenly Father.

As I neared the last stretch of road before turning onto our street, I felt I had finally run out of things to say. Then a question for Him came to my mind, so I asked: "God, what would you say to me on this, my fortieth birthday?"

I don't think I really expected Him to answer, but He did almost immediately and very clearly. I heard His voice say, *It's time to get to work. It's time to write your book.*

There it was again. Another reminder. This is what God had been calling me to do. I had started trying to put on paper the memories from a dreadful time of life that I had worked hard to block out. Tears quickly filled my eyes.

> People need to hear your story.

Hoping I wouldn't run into any of my neighbors, I quietly responded, "I feel like people probably get tired of hearing me talk about it."

People need to hear your story.

It was a brief conversation with my Heavenly Father, but the answer was clear. I have known for many years that I needed to write a book about our story. There has been this continual nudging of the Holy Spirit I cannot escape. There have also been many times when I shared a small bit of *those days* and strangers or acquaintances alike would say, "You need to write a book!"

With a little hesitation (and maybe even a bit of dread), I would say, "Yes, I know..."

I'm not sure why. I don't think my story is significant in any way. I can think of many others who have been through much worse than I have. I'm not sure how much of an impact I can make. Besides, who would even want to buy or read a book by me? Maybe a handful of family members or friends.

On one hand, this is a story of grief, pain, and bitterness—all the emotions that go hand-in-hand with death and loss. On the other hand, there have been undeniable miracles I have witnessed firsthand in my daughter along with the beautiful redemption story in which I so undeservedly was allowed to play a part. It was a time with such a strange mixture of emotions, trying to celebrate the birth of our sweet Sarah and every tiny step forward, mixed with the piercing dagger of grief remembering her twin sister, Alanna—the daughter we didn't get to bring home.

But if you sit down and have a conversation with any other person on the planet, they have a story, too—a story of a life full of events and circumstances that shaped the person they are now. Memories from years past where there was once joy and laughter and better times. Or memories of dark, sorrowful times when they can be thankful for where they are now. No two people have the same story. There may be similarities here and there, but we all struggle and react differently to the circumstances that come our way. No one is exempt from the heartache of loss, or the struggle of unexpected challenges and tragedies, yet we all *deal with it* or *handle it* in our own ways. My husband and I often refer to 2 Corinthians 1:3, 4 (NET), *Blessed is the God and Father of our Lord Jesus Christ, the Father of mercies and God of all comfort who comforts us in all our troubles so that we may be able to comfort those experiencing any trouble with the comfort with which we ourselves are comforted by God.*

We have not, nor will we ever *recover* or *get over* losing our daughter. What we do have to share is our story, a story of God's beautiful grace, lavished on us through it all. Our hope and prayer by putting our story into words is that we will bring comfort to those who are hurting, just as our Heavenly Father comforted us.

I was adding to the book a few days after my birthday reminder, and I had to stop as I had so many times before. It was a struggle to put into words the events of that time of my life, considering I had tried so hard to forget, to move on, to think about how well our daughter, Sarah, is doing now. My mom gave me a small notebook a day or two after the girls were born just in case I wanted to journal about those long days in the hospital. It was a thoughtful gift, but honestly, I didn't want to write anything down. I didn't want to remember this. I still don't want to remember the details of this horrible, traumatic time of my life. I still don't want to remember the pain or how many nights I spent crying myself to sleep. It hurts too much.

Now, every time I sit down to add to this story, memories come flooding back. The tears start flowing. The pain lumps in my throat. The ache throbs in my heart. It's like it just happened yesterday.

My mom kept a journal. My sister created a beautiful scrapbook using the journal entries with some pictures. Both have been tremendously helpful in putting the story together now.

For me, writing this story has been an extremely draining process. I've had to force myself to remember the stuff I once tried so hard to erase from my memory. Often, I stop for a cry break. Not with gentle tears rolling down my cheeks, but gut-wrenching, ugly sobs. The kind where you can't breathe, and your chest hurts, and you feel like your heart is going to burst with pain. Ask anyone who has lost someone dear to them. Some days the devastating loss of that loved one hits so hard that it feels as if the whole world just stops.

I don't want to do this, Lord. It's too hard. And if this is how it's going to be, I don't want to do it! It just hurts too much. I'm overwhelmed at this great feat. I don't understand why you have called me to do this. I am not a writer. I am not eloquent with words. I'm not good at this.

Although I didn't really ask for help, at that point something in me shifted, and I began to lean more on the Lord to help me. After all, if He asked me to do it,

He was going to have to help me do it. I think that's the point, though, right? If God only asks us to do stuff that we are great at, we don't really need Him for it.

It slowly became easier. When I recognize my shortcomings is when I can truly depend on the Lord for help. I constantly must remind myself that I am not doing this for me. When I feel stressed or don't know what to write, that's when I put it back in God's hands and say, "Even though I don't understand why you asked me to do this, I want to be obedient." I know there is a purpose to this task, whether it be for my own continued healing to put into words what the Lord has done for me, or if this is to help someone else who may be dealing with the same hurts and struggles.

I mentioned to Sarah one evening that I was going to be working on the book the next day.

"Oh, yeah, how's your book coming along?"

"Well, I haven't worked on it for a while because I just don't want to do it anymore, but I have to do it because God wants me to."

As she hugged me, she said, "God's plans aren't always our plans."

We continued discussing how God usually doesn't just ask us to do the fun, easy things we enjoy doing. Many times, He asks us to do the difficult things, things that push us, things that really make us dig down inside to see if our obedience to Him will only go so far—as long as the task is convenient and life isn't too hard.

My journey through loss, grief, and reconciliation has been a long process. Losing a child is something you just never get over. But, if I had written this story five years earlier, it wouldn't include the healing that has continued to take place in Sarah's life or my life throughout the years.

All I've Ever Wanted To Be

For as long as I can remember, I always looked forward to the day I would get to be a mom. As a young teenager, I often volunteered to help in the church nursery. I loved learning how to care for little ones and finding ways to make them laugh. And they seemed to like me, too. Although, once, a two-year-old I was babysitting locked me out of the house. Eventually, he unlocked the door, but that was the most terrifying ten minutes of my babysitting career. I hesitated to watch him again. However, it didn't scare me away for too long from what I knew I was created to be.

Holding a sleeping baby in your arms is heavenly. Just to look at a beautiful, perfectly created little person with chubby cheeks, soft skin, and their tiny fingers and toes is so precious. Hearing baby noises and jabbering in church or at a store always brings a smile to my face.

* * *

John and I met as eleven-year-old kids when his family moved to the small town of Holts Summit, just two-and-a-half miles from my house. We were both actively involved in our youth group and became good friends over the years. About halfway through our senior year of high school, he romantically hit me on the shoulder with his Bible and asked me to go with him to the youth group Valentine's banquet. We married just two-and-a-half years later. We worked hard, saved our money, and moved to Springfield, Missouri two years later for John to attend Central Bible College (CBC). Although I had a deep desire to be a mom, I knew this would have to wait until after John finished school.

While John was at CBC, we volunteered as youth leaders at a small church in Buffalo, Missouri. One night as John was leading the Bible study, he went around the room and had every person say what they wanted to be when they grew up.

> The only thing I've ever wanted to be is a mom.

I had never been able to answer that question. One semester at the local university right out of high school was all it took for me to realize I had no clue what to do next.

As the students around the room gave their responses, I struggled to think of any profession that I could toss out as a possibility, but nothing came to mind. So, in a moment of resolve at my turn I said, "The only thing I've ever wanted to be is a mom." I knew my life would never be complete until I became a mom. It was my calling, my purpose. But I had to wait a little longer.

During John's senior year at CBC, we decided it was time to start our family. For any woman trying to become pregnant, every strange feeling, every kind of sickness, any sign that something was a little off, brought on the hope that it just might be because of a baby. As the months went by with no results, each negative pregnancy test brought on a twinge of pain in my heart. There were several nights of crying myself to sleep, wondering if it would ever happen. *Were we ever going to be able to have children? Is there something wrong with me? Is it my fault?*

Being in our mid-twenties and having already been married for over five years, having a baby by then was expected. We would get the occasional, "So, when are you guys going to have kids?"

As I tried to talk around the lump in my throat, hoping I wouldn't tear up, the usual answers were something like, "We're just not ready yet," or "Hopefully someday."

For a woman wanting to conceive, yet not being able to, no matter how long you have been waiting, the emotion can immediately consume you in the moment of the simple question, "When are you going to have kids?" It can make you question everything about yourself, your worth, your success, your decisions, and your abilities. It made me feel like a failure. How do you respond to this question when you are constantly on the verge of an emotional breakdown?

I want to be a mom; I just can't be one right now. I guess it's not time yet.

And the months kept going by.

John graduated from CBC and accepted a position at the Assembly of God Church in Washington, Missouri. It was in Washington that I began talking with my chiropractor about my inability to conceive. After some brief testing, irregularities with my adrenal gland were discovered, which prevented me from having regular monthly cycles.

During this time, I also began discussing it all with my OBGYN, who prescribed the fertility medication, Clomid. We were hopeful that we were on the right track.

Only one month after taking the supplements recommended by my chiropractor, the fertility meds prescribed by my doctor, and using a fertility monitor daily, I found out I was pregnant. Finally! After waiting for so long, I was finally pregnant!

We met our parents for dinner at Colton's Steakhouse in Jefferson City and gave them their Valentine's Day cards with a special little note letting them know they were going to be grandparents. It was a joyous and exciting time, especially since this was going to be the first grandbaby!

Usually there were no weird cravings like I had always heard about in movies, but one night I told John I wanted a crunchy taco from Taco Bell, which was strange because it was something I hadn't had since I was a kid.

The day of our first ultrasound, when I was about eight weeks along, we were beyond excited to see our little one for the first time. As John and I sat waiting in anticipation for the image to come on the screen, we couldn't help but be a little anxious. The moment the ultrasound image came on the screen I looked over at John in shock. My doctor looked at me and asked if I could see what he was seeing and if I understood what it meant. We were stunned to see two little circles moving. We were having twins! YES! I had always wanted twins! We had talked about how great it would be to have twins because we felt like we were growing our family late in life so it would be a good way to catch up.

We were in love with them from the start. Being pregnant with twins put me at a higher risk, so we began having monthly ultrasounds. Just a few short weeks later, the ultrasound revealed that we were having two girls. It was all just so amazing and perfect. In the beginning, my pregnancy was fairly easy. I had some morning sickness, but nothing too bad. I rediscovered my love for chocolate milk during this time, as it helped settle my stomach and was a daily craving. Although, after telling my doctor this and apparently putting on too much weight too fast, I was told to cut back on the chocolate milk. But I didn't. Telling a pregnant woman to stop indulging in her craving is a dangerous thing to do.

My belly was growing fast. As much as I had looked forward to being a mom, nothing could have prepared me for the miraculous feeling of having two tiny humans growing inside my belly. It was amazing! It wasn't long before I began feeling uncomfortable and having some back pains, but I tried to keep moving. When I was almost five months pregnant, we took a vacation with my parents, driving from Missouri to North Carolina to visit my mom's brother, who lives near the beach. My dad drove the Winnebago, which was the only possible way for me to go because I could lie on the bed in the back if I got uncomfortable. It was a week full of memories and laughter with family I didn't get to see very often.

There is no beauty on earth that compares to being at the beach on a warm, sunny day. The sound of the waves crashing on the shore, the sand between my toes, and water lapping at my feet as we walked along the edge. My family had spent many vacations traveling to the beach, and it has always been my favorite place.

The beach was only a couple of miles away from my uncle's house. One day, I mentioned how much I missed being able to lie on my stomach. John took on the chore of digging out a belly-shaped hole in the sand for me so I could lie comfortably. He always takes such good care of me.

We made the long trip back home, but the next few weeks were full of traveling as well.

I went on a road trip with my mom and sister to a cousin's wedding in Lee's Summit, Missouri, and then we helped move John's grandma into her new apartment in Jefferson City, Missouri. John's family kept trying to get me to sit down to rest, but I felt good at the time and kept going.

I mention these events because in hindsight I often wonder if I overworked myself and caused what was about to happen.

The Day the Twins Were Born

The morning of June 16, 2008, I was in the kitchen washing dishes when I began feeling some unusual pain. After enduring the "pains" a few more times, I decided to call my OBGYN. I knew something wasn't right, but the nurse I spoke to told me to sit down for a while and it would probably go away. As the pain increased, I let John know that something was wrong and that I wanted to go to the doctor. I called the office again, and the nurse reluctantly scheduled me in for my own peace of mind. It wasn't until we pulled into the parking lot of the office that I realized the pain I had been feeling may have been contractions. I checked in and waited nervously for someone to call my name. It wasn't long before I was sitting on the exam table telling my OB what had been going on that morning. After a quick check, he informed me I was dilated to five centimeters, and they would be taking me to the hospital immediately.

John and my doctor walked with me as I was taken by wheelchair, through the long corridor connecting the offices to the hospital across the street. I wondered what in the world was going on. Was this really happening? At this point I was dilated too far to be able to stop the contractions. I was given medication to slow everything down just enough to prepare for delivery and transportation of the girls to a larger hospital. I was scared, but really had no idea what to expect or the gravity of the situation.

I was in somewhat of a fog for the next few hours as I tried to listen to a brief rundown of what to expect, make decisions about which hospital to send the girls, and who I wanted as a pediatrician. There was no time for an epidural, whether I wanted one or not. I hadn't even been given the chance to think about it yet. Within a couple hours, the delivery waiting room was full of family and friends, anxiously waiting for the girls' arrival. Two specialized teams from Children's Hospital in St. Louis came ready to transport the girls by helicopter. It was all happening so fast. The intimate, beautiful moment I had

The intimate, beautiful moment I had imagined for the delivery of our girls became one of fear and confusion.

imagined for the delivery of our girls became one of fear and confusion. I was unprepared for what was taking place, and I felt helpless.

The girls were coming fast, but I didn't know what to do because we never made it to any type of Lamaze or instructional class. I was only twenty-five weeks and four days along—barely halfway through my pregnancy. Looking back, I blame myself for being so ignorant that I didn't know I was having contractions. If I had known, I would have gotten to the hospital sooner. If I had known, I would have gone to the emergency room instead of wasting time trying to convince a nurse at the doctor's office that something was wrong. Maybe then, they would have been able to stop the contractions or at least been able to transport me to a hospital that was better equipped to take care of preemies.

* * *

Once the medical staff was set up and ready, the delivery began. At 5:00 pm, Sarah Nicole Jahnke was born weighing one-pound ten-and-a-half ounces and twelve-and-three-quarter inches long. She had a lot of bruising after getting stuck in the birth canal during delivery, and an episiotomy was necessary. A few minutes later at 5:07 pm, Alanna Grace Jahnke made her grand appearance weighing one-pound fourteen ounces and twelve-inches long.

All I could do was watch, trapped in that miserable hospital bed as our twins on opposite sides of the room were surrounded by medical professionals. Their lungs were extremely underdeveloped, which required them to be intubated immediately. This group of strangers were the first to hold and care for our babies. After carefully checking their vitals and placing them in Isolettes for transport, they slowly wheeled them by for us to see.

I didn't get to hold them. I didn't get to see my husband hold them. Nor did I get to pass them around to our parents, siblings, or friends. They were just gone, and the room was empty.

It was a crazy whirlwind of an afternoon, but as things settled down, we celebrated the birth of our girls with Hawaiian pizza from Papa John's, which became our tradition after each of our children's births. Our pastors and church friends came to visit. Before long, John went with some of our family to St. Louis Children's Hospital to be with the girls while I had to stay behind. And again, the room was empty.

* * *

I am forever grateful that my sister stayed with me that night. She slept on what I soon discovered was the most uncomfortable bed in existence—a hospital pull-out. I had given birth to two beautiful baby girls, but I didn't get to hold them before they were taken. I didn't sleep much as I laid in bed tossing, turning, and crying most of the night. I didn't want to be separated from them. I worried about them, wondering what was happening while I was 48.5 miles away. Yes, I know it's strange to know the exact distance, but later we discovered that to stay at the Ronald McDonald House—a place specifically for families whose children are in the hospital—you must live at least fifty miles from the hospital. We were shy a mere mile-and-one-half from the required distance.

It was a restless night. This was not the way it was supposed to be. I had dreamed of this moment for so long. The day your baby is born should be magical. Filled with joy. Surrounded by family. Holding your precious little one. But I felt so alone. I was worried. I was scared. And my arms were empty.

Because of the circumstances, my doctor came in at 5:00 am—the earliest possible—to release me. But it wasn't until about four hours later that I finally left St. Johns Mercy Hospital in Washington, Missouri, to go to St. Louis Children's Hospital to be with John and our babies. The girls each had her own room next to one another in the neonatal intensive care unit.

Sarah's and Alanna's first full day in the NICU was promising. They were both taken off their respirators and seemed to be doing well. However, Sarah had to remain under bili lights because of extensive bruising and jaundice.

Since everything seemed to be going well with the girls, we were finally able to celebrate the birth of the first grandbabies on both sides of the family with our parents and siblings. We took a short walk to a restaurant nearby. After all the uncertainty of the day before, we sat, laughed, and enjoyed being together.

When we got back, one of the first "mom" things I had the opportunity to do was to change Alanna's diaper. This seemingly simple task became a bit of a challenge for this tiny and fragile little girl. I had changed many babies' diapers before, but this was different. I was nervous and I felt clumsy. She was in a temperature-controlled container with two armholes, and she had tubes and wires attached all over her tiny body. Her skin was almost sticky because it was so underdeveloped. The nurses cautioned us to try not to rub the girls or touch their skin very often because it was painful for them. As a mom, I just wanted to be close to and hold my baby, but then I was told to try not to touch her? Allowed only to look through the glass at her? I spent many hours looking at my two micro-preemies—babies weighing less than one pound twelve ounces or before twenty-six weeks gestation at birth. My girls were born at twenty-five weeks and four days.

I had always planned to breastfeed my girls, but since that wasn't a possibility, I figured the next best thing was to pump milk so it would be ready when they were ready. I faithfully pumped every two to three hours, day and night for months. In the NICU there are "pumping rooms" available for moms for this very reason. To be on such a continuously strict schedule was draining, both mentally and physically. Many times, it was hard to pull myself away when we had family or friends visiting or when the girls were having various tests done. Yet, at the same time, it was also kind of an escape. In the middle of a noisy hospital filled with people talking and machines beeping non-stop, I shut myself away from it all and sat in silence in that tiny room. It was a place I could cry by myself, read the materials taped to the wall for the hundredth time, talk to God about what was happening, or, on occasion, fall asleep. I guess if you are tired enough, falling asleep while you are pumping is possible. I was so dedicated to the task, and the hospital was using so little, the staff eventually asked me to buy a freezer to store the milk at our house because my milk was taking over all of the NICU's freezer space.

The First Few Days

The day after the girls were born, a research group from Washington University asked if they could include our girls in a study they were conducting on preemies. We agreed, and within a few hours, they had hooked them each up to a machine to monitor their brain activity. As if there weren't already enough sensors attached to their tiny bodies, now their heads were completely covered. Even though I didn't understand all the data and numbers on the screen, I kept an eye on it to watch for any changes. I didn't say anything at the time, but I began to notice that Alanna's brain wave activity was decreasing.

St. Louis Children's Hospital has two or three tiny rooms in the NICU reserved for parents of the most critical babies. Nothing fancy, just a room with a bed, but it was close to our girls and allowed us some privacy and a little rest. We were blessed to be able to sleep there for the first few nights.

Sarah was the one they were worried about. In the middle of our second night, a nurse came and woke us up, needing permission to do a blood transfusion. They were both losing blood, but Sarah was more critical than Alanna.

We were called into the conference room the next day to discuss how sick the girls were. They were both suffering from brain bleeds—a condition called intraventricular hemorrhage, which is typical in premature babies because the blood vessels in their brains are extremely fragile. In the girls' cases, it was possibly caused by the helicopter rides from St. Johns Mercy Hospital in Washington, Missouri, where they were born, to St. Louis Children's Hospital. Their prognosis was not good. As time passed, the bleeding grew worse and was beginning to cause damage to the white matter in their brains. Each doctor reminded us at every visit that the girls were very sick. It was strange hearing the doctors say the girls were sick, when your idea of sickness is a cold, the flu, or some kind of infection.

> Each day, we begged God for good news, for signs of improvement, for anything positive. The news just kept getting worse...

Each day, we begged God for good news, for signs of improvement, for anything positive. The news just kept getting worse, and it was multiplied by two because they both were going through the same struggles. Both had to be put back on the ventilator, both needed more blood transfusions, both were having issues with bowel movements. But as time went on, hour by hour, they continued to slowly decline—bad reports, bad news. Yet we were still hopeful. We celebrated the small accomplishments, such as a wet diaper, which the staff called "liquid gold" because it indicated their organs were functioning properly. We trusted God to bring our girls through it all. I was scared, but my husband had faith that everything was going to be okay.

The Night Alanna Died

The girls were born on a Monday. On Thursday John and I were invited to a March of Dimes dinner for families with babies in the NICU. After all the stress and worry, we were kind of excited to get away for a little while for a nice dinner. However, now everything about that Thursday evening is so vivid with things I want to forget.... Things I try to forget.... Images I wish could be erased.

During dinner we exchanged stories with other parents and just tried to enjoy a good, free meal not cooked in the hospital cafeteria. We met another young couple with their three-year-old little boy who had been a preemie; yet here they were again after she delivered their second son prematurely. I became better acquainted with another mom later at the weekly meetups with the lactation consultant. We were able to get away from chaos and just sit and talk.

We hadn't been there too long when my dad rushed in, saying they needed us to come back to the room immediately. Something was wrong. As we hurried down the hall toward Alanna's room, our hearts dropped when we saw all the commotion in her room. The movable wall was pushed out to allow for all the people. The attending doctor as well as about seven or eight nurses and other medical staff surrounded our little girl.

To see a group of people administering CPR to your child is one of the most traumatic things a parent can see. They had already been trying to revive Alanna for twenty minutes while looking for John and me. As we walked in, some of the staff turned to look at us. We knew by the look on their faces that something was terribly wrong. The doctor said there was not much more they could do, but they would continue to try to revive her if we wanted.

> We would never get to see her smile or hear her voice or watch her play or hear her laugh ... I never knew how much my heart could hurt until that night.

Our immediate response was: *YES! Of course! Keep trying!* But as we watched for a few more minutes, helplessly, hopelessly, pleading to God to save our little girl, we realized she was not going to make it. The attending doctor looked at us one more time to let us know they had done all they could, but that it was time to stop. The nurses began removing the feeding tube, breathing tubes, and all other cords attached. Then we finally held our little Alanna for the very first time as she died. We would never know what color her eyes were. We would never get to see her smile or hear her voice or watch her play or hear her laugh.

We sat in disbelief, in horror, in utter brokenness, holding our baby. I never knew how much my heart could hurt until that night. I held her, then John, then our parents. She had a brain hemorrhage, her air passage was blocked, and her organs had shut down.

I don't remember much of what happened between then and as I lay in bed that night. A nurse came in to take some pictures of us with her. How do you prepare for that? Living in the hospital NICU, you don't spend a lot of time or effort fixing your hair or dressing up. I was only a few days out from giving birth, so I was still wearing baggy clothes and putting my hair in a simple ponytail. I took a minute to check my hair, but how do you prepare to take pictures with your baby that has just died? Changing my clothes or putting on makeup seemed so pointless.

One of the nurses found a preemie outfit somewhere in the unit to put on Alanna because we didn't have clothes for her yet. It was a striped pastel onesie that was huge on her tiny, frail body. The nurses were so kind to help us during those moments. I never would have thought of taking pictures at a time like that, but those are the only pictures we have of her face with nothing attached to it. It's so strange remembering the details of those few hours that night, yet at the time it all felt so unreal—like some sort of horrible nightmare.

There was a room reserved in the NICU for parents whose baby just died. It was spacious but sterile and cold, and we had our own bathroom, which was a bit of a luxury for us at the time. I don't remember much once we got to the room. I remember John wrapping me in his arms trying to bring comfort while we lay in bed that night.

The one thing I do remember is the very brief conversation I had with God as I cried myself to sleep: *How dare you betray me like this.*

* * *

No one wants to plan a funeral for their child. Yet here we were, faced with this dreadful task. How did it come to this? Just days ago, life was full of hope for the future of our family with the coming addition of twin girls. In a matter of days, that joy turned into a dreadful nightmare. There were decisions that needed to be made: where to bury her, picking out a tombstone design, what to dress her in, and other details I didn't want to think about. We hadn't even decorated a nursery for her. We hadn't bought toys or clothes or blankets yet, and now we never would. And on top of it all, our other child was in the hospital fighting for her life.

A sweet couple from our church owned a funeral home. They helped walk us through all the decisions we had to make. I can still picture that conference room in the hospital where we met with Bill as he sat across the table from us. We decided to have a small graveside ceremony with only family and pastors, in Jefferson City, near where we grew up. I had never seen an infant coffin before. It was so strange. John's grandma made a beautiful little dress for Alanna to be buried in because everything was way too big on her tiny body. There we laid our baby's body to rest in the infant section of the cemetery.

Several people wanted us to have a second, larger ceremony for friends and people from our church to be able to come and show their love and support for us. Originally, we had thought about doing something down the road when Sarah was more stable, but when that time came it just didn't feel right. We didn't really want to go through that process again. Even though we had received so many bad reports those first few days, we truly believed that everything was going to be okay in the end. But after Alanna died, there was the looming fear that we were going to lose Sarah, too. She was just as sick as Alanna had been. My heart ached so much after losing one, the thought of losing both was unbearable. I found myself pleading with God out of desperation. *God, what am I going to do if Sarah dies, too? Please don't take both of my babies!*

Sarah was still in such a critical condition that we couldn't be away from the hospital for too long, just in case...

Generosity

The outpouring of love and support we received was, without a doubt, the most amazing display of giving I had ever experienced in my life. We were overwhelmed with cards of prayer and encouragement—sometimes from people we didn't even know. Gifts of money, gas cards, food cards, and meals were left at the church for us to pick up. It was humbling and so amazing to know people all over Missouri and even churches in other states were constantly praying for us and our little girl. I looked forward to those who brought meals to us or visited us at the hospital because we would get to take them to meet Sarah. They were always amazed at how tiny she was. With some laughter and some tears, we shared brief updates of her current progress or struggles, and they prayed over her and us at the end. I cherished the times of talking face-to-face with a friend.

At the risk of sounding ungrateful, please bear with me. While I appreciated every card from kind, well-intentioned, and loving individuals who took the time to write to us, I couldn't bring myself to read the cards. John read them aloud to me. But anytime a scripture verse was mentioned, I shut down. Thank you for the prayers, but I didn't really want to hear about "how good God is" right then.

Finding Routine and Rough Days

As the weeks dragged on and John returned to work, we settled into a routine that lasted for the next three months. I stayed at the hospital Monday through Thursday; then went home for a night. Together, we returned to the hospital to stay Friday and Saturday; then went home again to attend our church on Sunday; all to begin the cycle again the next day.

The days living in a hospital were tough. I made sure to be in Sarah's room first thing in the morning while the doctors and interns were making their rounds, usually between 6:30 and 7:30 am. We were lucky enough to have a room with a recliner, where I spent many restless nights. Beeping machines and nurses coming into the room—seemingly every twenty minutes—checking vitals, feeding her, drawing blood, or many other countless things they checked led to nights of little sleep. Although I didn't understand a lot of what they said, at least I was there to ask questions, hear how she was doing from their perspective, and see what the plan was moving forward.

From the day the girls were born, we were told to expect two steps forward and one step back; and that we would most likely be there until the original due date, which was September 25, 2008. (They were born on June 16th.) The unsettledness of making some progress for a couple of days only to hear a bad report the next was exhausting.

Sarah would breathe well one day; they would turn her oxygen down; then the next day she struggled, and the oxygen would have to be turned back up. She would gain a few ounces here and there, and then lose a little. As parents who just wanted to take our baby home, we were hopeful at times that she would be ahead of schedule. Unfortunately, we had to be there for the long haul.

The hospital had several areas especially for families with ill children admitted long-term. One was a designated waiting room for families staying overnight. There were chairs for the day that doubled as pull-out beds—with sheets, blankets, and pillows to help families get some much-needed rest at night. While it was good to lie down instead of propped up in a recliner, these pull-outs were not the most comfortable, but the room was quiet and dark. Some days we spent in the Ronald McDonald room—a place for NICU families daytime use with snacks, some comfy furniture, a larger space to hang out when family or friends came to visit, a computer to use, and a TV. Hidden on another floor was a lovely garden for times to just get some fresh air.

Even with these little getaways, I found it very difficult to leave Sarah's side even for a short time because of the constant fear of missing something when she needed me close.

The nurses and staff at Children's Hospital were so friendly and helpful. We had a favorite nurse, Jen, who was with Sarah regularly. She knew us, and most of all, she knew Sarah.

Sarah had quite a reputation around the NICU. She was feisty; she was a fighter; and she did not like people messing with her. After changing her diaper or taking blood samples, the nurses swaddled her to keep her still and to prevent her from grabbing the sensors or tubes. Within a matter of minutes, she would kick one leg free from the blanket. She pulled her CPAP (Continuous Positive Airway Pressure) mask off a couple of times, and pulled out her feeding tube. She constantly knocked the heartbeat and oxygen sensors off. Anytime a new nurse came to take care of Sarah,

Sarah had quite a reputation around the NICU. She was feisty; she was a fighter; and she did not like people messing with her.

I told them a little about her. They would say, “Oh, we know about Sarah.”

* * *

We had a few fantastic nurses who rotated in taking care of our girl, but every now and then a new nurse would be on duty. On this particular Saturday, the nurse was new. My mom and sister came to the hospital for a visit that day. Sarah was about two-and-a-half months old, and she was on a nasal cannula. Her breathing had been improving daily. But for some reason, Sarah’s oxygen levels kept dropping throughout this day. We told the nurse on duty about it, but she didn’t seem to be very concerned.

Although nothing significant was happening, as the day went on, we had a growing concern that something was wrong. It was disheartening because she had been doing so well, but suddenly that day, her breathing became more of a struggle. We stayed close to her all day, praying, talking, watching, alerting the nurse. About 4:00 pm, after convincing the nurse that something wasn’t normal, she finally began to check the device and discovered that a connection to the oxygen tank had come loose.

While it was a relief to discover it was just a problem with the machine, I also realized the importance to stay aware, notice inconsistencies, and speak up, even if it means telling the nurse several times that something is wrong. It makes me sad to think about how much Sarah struggled that day, but also thankful that it was discovered and corrected when it was.

* * *

With all her complications, medications needed, and machines helping to keep her alive, Sarah needed only one surgery that took place when she was two weeks old. Patent ductus arteriosus—a common occurrence in premature babies—is a heart defect where a vein that normally closes at birth stays open. PDA ligation is typically considered a minor procedure; however, Sarah being so unstable made the decision much more complicated. Putting her under anesthesia was a scary risk but needed to be done. She still bears the scar from the stitches on her back. The original incision was about two inches; yet the scar has grown with her and is now about six inches long.

Talking to Sarah through her glass cage wasn't enough. I just wanted her to feel the love I had for her. It was a full three weeks after the girls were born before I was finally able to hold our little Sarah for the first time. And, boy, was it an ordeal! Because of her condition, we were limited to one person holding her for one hour once a week. Two nurses had to be there to move the wires and machinery around. I sat in the recliner and anxiously waited for them to place her on my chest.

When I finally got to hold my Sarah, I was afraid to move or breathe or even talk. There she lay, this tiny, less than two pounds of skin and bones little girl, eyes still sealed shut, sensors attached all over her head and chest, unable to make any sound because of the breathing tube down her throat. I wanted to hold her close, wrap my arms around her, and kiss her head. But she was too small to cuddle, and her head was covered with the sensors for the brainwave study. She just lay there, sleeping. One hour wasn't enough, but it was all I got. The hour flew by, but I cherished every second.

The next week was John's turn. I loved watching him hold our baby and sing over her. He was an amazing dad from the start, and so natural at it. A nurse helping that day took a picture of us all together. It was our first family picture, and it's one of my favorites.

Gradually, as she became stronger, we were able to hold her more often for longer periods of time. Sarah slept for most of the time when we held her. Occasionally, when she was finally able to open her eyes, she would be awake and just look at us, not making a sound. We would just get to be together. We needed each other. It was like a little bit of my heart healed with each minute I held her. I'm pretty sure she loved being held even though she couldn't tell me. Sometimes, we would fall asleep holding her. I felt a little guilty about falling asleep holding her because our time together was so short. But I often imagined that is what we would be doing if we were home together—you know, if things were the way they were supposed to be.

Going Home

On October 1, 2008, after living in the hospital for 107 days, we finally brought our sweet girl home! Weighing just over six pounds, she was able to hold her body temperature and pass the car seat test—she had to be able to keep her breathing at a good rate while buckled into a car seat for an allotted amount of time. The only thing holding her back was she was still on a feeding tube. Since we had proven ourselves responsible parents by being present and caring for our daughter, they trained us to properly use, insert, and remove the feeding tube. Once Sarah was home, she took a bottle very well, and we removed the feeding tube within a couple of days.

All the diagnoses wrapped in this tiny bundle brought on a lot of uncertainty of the future. Although we were ready to bring her home, we had no idea of the challenges we would face. The possibility of many long-term effects of her extreme prematurity weighed heavily on us as new parents. Even though she was three-and-a-half months old, it had been the hospital staff who had taken on the bulk of her care. We were bringing home a baby with chronic lung disease, possible brain damage, an eye disease typical in preemies, and constant issues with milk aspiration. She would be at high-risk for apnea, infections, sicknesses, and would most likely need physical and occupational therapy. She would be delayed one year for every month she was born early, meaning since she was born three-and-a-half months early, it would take three-and-a-half years to catch up to other children her age. We were filled with mixed emotions as we said goodbye to the NICU staff and left the hospital to go home with our baby for the first time. With this joy, though, came the reminder as we passed the room where Alanna had once stayed that we were bringing only one little girl home.

John drove while I sat in the back seat with Sarah, not once taking my eyes off her.

Home. We would finally get to experience some form of normalcy like other families taking a new baby home for the first time.

Pretending

A couple of weeks after bringing Sarah home from the hospital, we began attending church every Sunday and Wednesday. Back to the routine. Time to show everyone that I'm okay. We're okay. Everything was back to normal.

John had been a pastor for only a couple of years at the time of our loss. While I never went to Bible school, trying to fill the role of a *pastor's wife* was a bit of a struggle for this ordinary girl with no qualifications. I had this idea of what a *pastor's wife* should look like, be like, and act like. The model of a perfect Christian lady who knows what to say at the right time, what to do during difficult circumstances, and is a strong leader for the women's group of the church. I assumed this kind of unspoken rule that if you are in ministry, you have achieved a perfect relationship with God and an understanding of Him that nothing could shake.

When John was still in Bible college, I began contemplating what my role would be someday, and a feeling of complete inadequacy crept in. I became aware that I was not equipped to be a *pastor's wife*. I felt like a fraud holding a position for which I was completely unqualified. One thing was for certain, I couldn't let anyone know what was really going on inside.

There were days I just wanted someone to talk to—someone who didn't know me or my husband or that I was married to a pastor; someone who wouldn't preach at me or say to read the Bible more. I didn't need someone to tell me to just have faith and believe that God will work it all out. I felt so alone. I didn't even talk to my husband about my inner struggles, although, I'm sure to a degree he felt my struggles.

> I felt like a fraud ... One thing was for certain, I couldn't let anyone know what was really going on inside.

I couldn't tell anyone how I really felt. How would it look if the pastor's wife was questioning her faith? Would it affect my husband's job? What church wants a pastor whose wife is angry at God? I decided to keep it all to myself and walk through this alone. I needed to figure it out on my own. I was there, but I didn't want to be. Everything was not okay, but I had learned to put on a happy face, pretend that everything was okay, and show the church we were moving forward.

Having a baby that had just spent three-and-a-half months in the NICU gave me the perfect excuse I needed to limit my interaction with people in the church. I kept her with me during the service until she was well over a year old. She was a needed distraction during the singing and preaching. We carried on with our new little one, thankful she was okay, glad she was finally home, and we could move away from the awfulness of living part-time in a hospital. And while everything seemed fine on the outside, on the inside I would never be the same.

I had not experienced any type of devastating tragedy for those first twenty-eight years of my life. My life had been easy. I grew up with two loving parents who raised me in church. I don't ever remember a time in need of anything while growing up. My parents had decent-paying jobs with benefits. We took vacations every summer, usually to a beach. We had a home, food on the table, clothes on our backs; as far as I knew, everything we needed.

I thought I knew enough about God. After all, I had heard thousands of messages, Bible stories, and songs about Him Sunday mornings, Sunday nights, Wednesday nights, church camps, youth conventions, and different retreats for twenty-eight years. Yet suddenly, I didn't know Him at all. How could He do this to me? After Alanna's death, the truths that I had depended on all my life came into question. The faith I had in an all-knowing, all-powerful God was gone.

During the time we were trying to get pregnant I remember singing a song about a Savior who could move the mountains. This was my declaration that my God who can move mountains would help us to be able to have a baby. Then while pregnant, I sang this as a song of praise to God for moving my mountains. But after we lost Alanna, it took years for me to be able to sing the song.

The loss of our daughter forced me to face what I thought I knew about God and who I truly believed He was. I grew up believing in the God who worked miracle after miracle for an ungrateful nation. I was always frustrated with them because of their lack of faith and constant turning away from God. It was a seemingly obvious cycle to me as the reader: the times they followed God they were blessed, and the times they turned from Him they were punished. In the Old Testament, God was strict, demanding, and required allegiance. But then, Jesus came to earth, lived a sinless life, died on a cross for our sins, was raised to life after three days, and now God is gracious and forgiving.

I knew the stories. I sang the songs. I could even quote a bunch of Bible verses. But now, everything was different. We had prayed for our girls, our church had prayed for our girls, the church our parents attended had prayed for our girls, people all over the country had prayed for our girls, but for some reason, it wasn't enough. God could have intervened, He could have healed Alanna, He could have kept me from delivering prematurely. But He didn't. He was silent. Where was He? The time I needed Him the most and He wasn't there. He was silent.

There was no question in my mind that God existed.

The evidence of a Creator is overwhelming. There is no way that life in all its complexities could have happened by accident. To me, the idea that everything started from an explosion or by chance or that everything came about by the tiniest organism evolving over millions of years to somehow create plants and animals and humans is completely absurd. I have never in my life doubted the existence of God. An infinitely creative designer is the only plausible explanation for our world.

> I have never in my life doubted the existence of God ... What I did question was his care and love for me.

What I did question was His care and love for me. While He is the creator of all things, I began to believe that He was not concerned with answering my prayers. Sure, I had seen and heard stories of answered prayer, of modern-day miracles, but He didn't do them for me. He didn't love me enough. He didn't care for me enough to answer my prayers. All the time I had spent serving Him meant nothing because now He was silent.

I believed in God. I just no longer believed He cared about me. I was angry at Him, and I didn't want anything to do with Him, nor did I want to go to church. But I had to be there. After all, my husband was the Associate Pastor. I was the Associate Pastor's wife. I had to stand strong, to show everyone that I was still trusting, still believing in God for miracles for Sarah, yet grieving like a good Christian girl when people would say something like, "You'll get to see her again someday when we're all in heaven together." I felt expected to put on a happy face, nod in agreement, muster up a smile, hold it all in, and show them that I was okay.

But I wasn't okay. On the inside, I was not the same.

The emptiness you feel after the loss of a child can be absolutely unbearable. My heart hurt so bad. Then to compound that with the loss of faith in the God I had served my whole life, it was as if I could physically feel my heart harden. For anyone who has lost a child, whether it be by miscarriage, infant loss, or some tragedy in life, the absence is felt for the rest of your life, at least to some degree. Every milestone they miss, every birthday and holiday, not getting to watch them grow, not getting to hold them, not getting to see them. It's a constant thought of what they would look like now, what they would be doing now. It doesn't go away. Some days it is easier, but then there are *those* days—the ones that hit hard. A scene in a movie, a picture, a small reminder of the loss, and it hits you like a train, and the tears start flowing, the heart aches again.

The God of the universe had *betrayed me*—words ingrained in my mind forever. Words, *How dare you betray me like this?* spoken out of pain, loss, and desperation. The God I thought I knew had finally shown Himself to me. Or rather chose not to. He had lost my trust.

I realized that I had developed a particular reaction to bad circumstances. If something bad happened, I would throw up a little prayer, and then hold my breath hoping for the best.

There is a song that reminds me so much of this time of my life. One line in particular says, "Jesus, you don't owe me anything."[1] Growing up knowing about God, going to church faithfully, doing everything I thought I was supposed to do, I had the idea that I had put in my time, I had earned the right for God to save my baby. We never skipped church for sports, school activities, or just because we were tired after a long day.

Yes, I felt like He had owed me.

Blaming

The morning I went into labor has been replayed in my mind hundreds, if not thousands of times. What could I have done differently? How did it all go so wrong?

For a long time, I was angry at the nurse who I had to convince to make an appointment for me that morning. I didn't know I was having labor pains, but she should have known what was going on. If she had only allowed me to come in when I first called, surely it would have been early enough to stop the contractions.

What about my doctor? What if he had made a different call concerning a helicopter? We learned later that one risk of life-flighting a preemie is it can cause brain bleeds. Would it have helped if I had been taken by ambulance to deliver at St. Louis Children's Hospital? Then, at least I wouldn't have been separated from my girls that first night.

The night Alanna died when we had gone to the March of Dimes dinner, could something have happened differently had we been in her room instead of at the dinner? What if we had chosen the other hospital in St. Louis to send the girls? Would they have been able to save Alanna?

Why did God allow one to live and not the other? Was there a reason? Was God punishing me for something I did? Was He still angry at me for something I had done in the past?

What went wrong in my body that caused me to deliver too early? Was my body just not able to take care of the precious tiny girls in my womb any longer? As much as I wanted to find someone to blame, sometimes things just happen. With no other explanation as to what caused my preterm labor, I eventually concluded that my body just couldn't carry them any longer. That realization brought on guilt and shame that would haunt me for many years. It was my fault.

There is a deep desire in all of us to search for a reason why something has happened. We feel the need to find someone or something to blame. When faced with hardships or circumstances we don't understand, the natural reaction is to ask *why*?

Just spend a little time with someone who has kids. Try to have a normal conversation and see the number of times their child/children come to ask them questions. It is nonstop. My kids are getting older, yet there are times when I am speaking when my son breaks into the middle of my sentence to start talking to me. I needfully remind him, *Words are coming out of my mouth right now. You're going to have to wait to ask your question until I finish my sentence.*

As a mom, when I give instructions to my kids, they often respond with: "Why?" The *why* questions usually come after I've given instructions that they disagree with. Sometimes I want to say, *"I am your mother and when I tell you to eat your vegetables, by golly, you'd better eat your vegetables. Why? Because I said so."* But the real reason is because even though you would rather get straight to dessert, as would I, there is value in the nutritional aspect of eating healthy foods. Because I don't want you to struggle with diabetes when you get older; because fruits and vegetables help your eyesight, your memory, your heart, your immune system, and can lower the risk of cancer. As an adult, I know a little more than you do about how your body works and how what you eat now will affect how healthy you will be later in life. When you are hungry twenty minutes before dinner is ready, the snack you want is not always what you need.

When you have multiple kids, much of your life is spent answering questions, waiting for someone to finish going to the bathroom, or making sure all things are divided equally. Counting the chips, crackers, or peanut butter cups to make sure everyone has the same number, because heaven forbid that one kid has more M&M's than another. It takes up a lot of energy. After years of doing this, I got tired of counting. I said, "Kids, as much as Daddy and I try to make everything fair and equal for you, life is not always going to be this way. Life is not fair. Someone is going to get more cookies than you. People are going to be mean. You're going to lose a game because the other team cheated. You'll get blamed and get in trouble for things you didn't do because someone lied. You are going to have to deal with the consequences of another's wrong choices. Life is not fair."

Life is not fair.

Children expect mom or dad to come to the rescue when there's a bully on the playground. Mom must be the one to cut the last brownie into parts so everyone gets the same size. Dad becomes the judge when an argument over the rules threatens to ruin the game. We can step in to make sure justice prevails over these situations.

But then, the unfair things, such as a false and slanderous accusation that causes the loss of a job, or the purchase of a house with costly hidden problems, or the death of a loved one because of a drunk driver cause us to cry out for someone to come rescue us from this injustice! Now it becomes God's problem to fix.

Why did God let that happen? Why does God heal some people and not others? Why did that person get the promotion or job over me? God, you could have prevented, you could have healed, you could have fixed…but you didn't. You chose not to intervene. The questions can shift from people being unfair to wondering about God's fairness. Somehow, we think if we just knew why, it could ease the pain.

Finding God: Job

What do you do when you find yourself in a place questioning everything you thought you knew about God? I began a reluctant journey, trying to determine what I really believed. I have never been much of a reader. I had read the Bible through as a requirement to complete the girls' Christian program I was in as a child, but other than that, most of my Bible knowledge came from listening to sermons on Sunday morning or Wednesday evening at my church.

The Bible is a *big* book! There are thousands of years of history and lots of cultural references that only a Jewish scholar would know. I was intimidated at the thought of reading and figuring things out on my own.

My biblical knowledge was limited to what I had been taught by someone else. I always thought that studying the Bible was just too difficult for someone like me. I am a numbers person. I love algebra. In math you get a problem, you use a formula, you find the answer. It makes sense. I am terrible at reading a text, analyzing the meaning, picking up on clues and the point the writer is trying to communicate. I just never got it. I've never felt smart enough. Even when faced with the task of writing this book, I've been afraid to let the world know just how limited I am and for people to find out that I'm not very smart.

But I could not escape the drawing I felt in my spirit to read the Bible. Where did I start, you may ask. The book of Job. I know it sounds strange. At the time, I didn't really want to read it, but I was looking for answers. And where better to start than with someone else who had dealt with loss. Job starts out with the story of a man described as *blameless and upright* who lost everything—an unbelievable tragedy, the death of all ten of his children, his servants, his cattle and sheep and camels—and finally even his own health was compromised. Yet Job 1:22 NKJV, says, "In all this Job did not sin nor charge God with wrong."

> In my heart I had turned away from God. I no longer cared what He thought, what He wanted, what He had to say...

My struggle with God was never public. I didn't tell my family and others that everything they taught me growing up was a lie, that none of it mattered anymore.

Nor did I negate all the Bible verses shared with me about God's love and care for me. I smiled and nodded. I didn't tell them my real thoughts nor that their words were just falling on deaf ears. Yet in my heart I had turned away from God. I no longer cared what He thought, what He wanted, what He had to say about the matter. Did I sin? I never purposefully did wrong to get back at Him or show Him I didn't care, but I did *charge Him with wrongdoing.* While I never believed God caused the death of my child, I held to the fact that by not healing her, He chose to let her die. And for that, He was no longer a god I wanted to serve. By not doing what He should have done, He was in the wrong. That was something I couldn't forgive.

After the initial tragedy in the story, reading the book of Job kind of dragged on. Thirty-six chapters of discussions between Job and his friends seemed so irrelevant, and I'll admit, I didn't really get anything out of it. That is until I read the heading over chapter 38: "God Answers Job." Now that caught my attention. I had grown up hearing people say things like "the Lord spoke to me" or "I feel like God is telling me…" or "This is what the Lord wants me to tell you." I was sure that it happened. I believed their stories. It just had never happened to me. That was something that only happened to super-spiritual people. If God was going to respond, why did He wait so long? Why did He allow Job's friends to go *on* and *on*?

GOD ANSWERS JOB

Now, maybe I can find something useful to help me understand why God allowed this to happen. I was hoping for a "God answers Stephanie" moment. Yet His response wasn't the response I was expecting. It wasn't a direct answer. God didn't answer with a booming voice of scolding or constant reprimand. Rather it was a series of questions. Lots of questions. Directed back at Job.

> 1 Then the Lord answered Job from the whirlwind:
> 2 "Who is this that questions my wisdom
> with such ignorant words?
> 3 Brace yourself like a man,
> because I have some questions for you,
> and you must answer them.
> 4 "Where were you when I laid the foundations of the earth?
> Tell me, if you know so much.
> 5 Who determined its dimensions
> and stretched out the surveying line?
> 6 What supports its foundations,
> and who laid its cornerstone
> 7 as the morning stars sang together
> and all the angels shouted for joy?
> 8 "Who kept the sea inside its boundaries
> as it burst from the womb,
> 9 and as I clothed it with clouds
> and wrapped it in thick darkness?

10 For I locked it behind barred gates,
limiting its shores.
11 I said, 'This far and no farther will you come.
Here your proud waves must stop!'
12 "Have you ever commanded the morning to appear
and caused the dawn to rise in the east? Job 38:1-12 (NLT)

After all, God says, *"You know all this! For you were born before it was all created...!"* Job 38:21 (NLT)

From there, God continues with questions about the weather, constellations, different animals, and how they care for their young. Eventually Job realizes his folly and resolves to speak no more. And then in Job 40:8 (NLT), God asks Job an interesting question: *"Will you discredit my justice and condemn me just to prove you are right?"*

There are different ways to read God's response, and it all hinges on how you view God. Do you view Him as an angry God with a quick temper, always ready to condemn? To be honest, that's kind of how I viewed God most of my life—easily angered and ready to punish me after each mistake. Reading the passage with that type of understanding will paint God as unsympathetic and distant. As if God was mad at Job daring to question Him, so He becomes snarky and sarcastic because He is easily offended by our questions: *I know how things work and you don't, so you need to sit down and be quiet.*

The Lord answered Job out of a whirlwind. This gives us a picture of a storm with noisy, rushing wind. If there was a crazy storm, then God must have been yelling, right? But that's not what's happening. We find out just a few chapters later that the Lord wasn't angry at Job because he was the one who spoke the truth about Him. Job 42:7.

On the other hand, if you see God as the omniscient creator that He is and as the only one who can answer all the questions regarding earth's natural order, who speaks and teaches with authority and complete understanding, as someone ready to have a conversation with you, the passage has quite the different feel. God wasn't showing off His knowledge to shame Job—just the opposite. It was a display of His intimate involvement in creation and His caring and watchful eye for all living creatures. He let Job know that He is aware of what is happening all around us, not just what consumes us, but every bit of His creation.

Try reading it both ways and see for yourself the difference varied perceptions have on reading it.

* * *

When bad things happen, we tend to ask God *why*? I don't understand why things happened the way they did. Why wasn't I able to carry my twins to full term, or at least to a point where they could be delivered safely? Why didn't God answer our prayers to heal Alanna?

And now, all these years later, Sarah has been asking me the same questions. "Why did God choose to heal me and not my sister?" "Why am I different?" "Why are things harder for me?"

As early as we could, we talked about Alanna to our children. We never wanted them to *find out* that they had a sister. It has brought about many conversations about heaven—what it's like, what Alanna could be doing, what she would look like. Most of the time tears are shed. These are hard questions to grapple with on my own. How am I supposed to teach my children when I don't have the answers myself? One thing I have learned is, if I gave them control, the questions swirling around in my mind would drive me crazy! One day during the questioning, the thought came to me, *If you knew the answer, would it help?* It stopped me in my tracks. The answer is obviously, *No, it wouldn't help because knowing why will never bring her back.*

* * *

What I believe God was trying to show Job is that the answers to our questions aren't as simple as we would like them to be. We see such a small portion of the whole. When tragedy strikes, we see ourselves at the center of creation, which makes our pain more important than everything around us. This means everything else revolves around us, and even God's will and purpose must bend to our will. We become so consumed with our own lives that we forget we can't see everything. While it wasn't evident at the time, I can see now how self-absorbed I was in my grief. I loved my husband but very rarely (if at all) asked him how he was doing. Grief can be so consuming that the assumption is: *no one is hurting as much as me.*

"Who is able to advise the Spirit of the Lord? Who knows enough to give him advice or teach him?" Isaiah asks in 40:13 (NLT).

> "My thoughts are nothing like your thoughts," says the Lord. "And my ways are far beyond anything you could imagine. For just as the heavens are higher than the earth, so my ways are higher than your ways and my thoughts higher than your thoughts." Isaiah 55:8-9 (NLT).

We want a simple answer to make us feel better after terrible injustices. We feel like God owes us an explanation. If God is just, how could He have allowed this to happen? The truth is that there is no easy answer. Part of God's response to Job in 40:8 (NLT) is: *"Will you discredit my justice and condemn me just to prove you are right?"*

So, if what we want or think should happen, doesn't happen, does that automatically mean God did something wrong? Is it possible for bad things to happen and God still be just? If we know what's best, are we condemning God as the one in the wrong?

* * *

There are other instances in the Bible when prophets in the Old Testament questioned God about how He was dealing with things that were happening at the time. Just as in the book of Job, there are sections in Jeremiah and Habakkuk when the prophets ask God questions and God answers back! Granted, God's answers aren't necessarily what we want to hear. In paraphrase, His answers go a little something like this:

- *It's not time yet.* Habakkuk 2:3
- *I'm about to do something, but you're not going to believe it, even if I tell you.* Habakkuk 1:5
- *If you think this is bad, what are you going to do when things get a whole lot worse?* Jeremiah 12:5
- *I am taking care of it even though you can't see how.* Jeremiah 12:14-17
- *Trust me and I will take care of you through the hard times.* Jeremiah 17:7-8
- *I will restore you.* Jeremiah 16:15

In our pain and lack of understanding, we cry out:
Why, God?
How, God?
When, God?

We want the quick answer, the easy out, the smoothest path because we don't want to have to deal with the pain for very long. *Give me something to make this easi-*

er. Give me a way to take back control of whatever it was I lost control of; I need a quick way to fix this.

The flaw here is that we never really had control in the first place, which is the scary part. We can think that we are in control of our lives, that is until the unexpected happens and we can't do anything about it. We can do everything in our power that we know to do, and it will never be enough. We can do everything right, and still fail. There will still be tragedy and heartache.

So where do we go from here?

Why should I trust God to be the one in control of my life? Why should I trust Him now, after all that's happened?

When I was a teenager, many road trips were spent listening to a cassette of Mark Lowry—a Christian comedian, singer, songwriter, and one of my favorite storytellers. As he retold the story of a terrible accident he had been in, he recounted how several people had asked him why God allowed it to happen. "I knew I'd heard it said, 'You don't ask God why accusatively, but I heard you can ask God why inquisitively.'"[2] When we ask *why* accusatively, we are really saying, "God, I need to speak to you about your justice. This isn't fair and You made a wrong decision in how you handled it. You really messed up this time."

God doesn't even give Job an answer why because the questions themselves weren't the heart of the issue. In all of God's questions to Job, He established that if

Job didn't understand the most common occurrences in nature, how could he even begin to understand how God works in our daily lives.

If you are waiting for me to tell of the moment God revealed to me why He allowed our daughter to die, I hate to break it to you, but He never told me.

What I began to realize was that no simple answer would ever be enough to satisfy my longing to understand why this happened. Because, if I'm honest, it wasn't about why it happened, it was why did God *let* it happen, which is a completely different question.

Horrible things happen every day, which is unfortunately part of life, but the struggle as a believer in an all-powerful God is understanding why He acts in some situations but not in others. How does He make the decision who to heal and who to let die?

What was exposed in me was a critical flaw that I didn't even realize was there. I had the expectation that "If I do this, then God must do that." I did my part by attending church and believing in You, now You are supposed to keep up Your end of the bargain by doing what I want. These deep cracks in the foundation of my understanding of what it means to have a relationship with God were being revealed. When I was a teenager, the big push in the church world was, *It's not about religion, it's a relationship.* It was this contrast between just going to church and being a rule-follower to building a personal relationship with God. But the foundation of my relationship with God was still based on trying to be good and do all the right things so that He wouldn't be mad at me. It was a fear-based relationship. I had to stay obedient so I wouldn't end up in hell.

Could any small adjustment in the series of events that led up to Alanna's birth and death changed the outcome? Maybe. Can I expect the Almighty Creator to spare me from hardship? I believe He has answered prayers and protected me in lots of ways that I don't even know about. Can I expect that He will spare me from *every* heartache?

What God reveals to us in His "answers" is that He does see what is happening all around us and that He is working. We think we need to know all the hows and whys and whens, but in the Father's infinite wisdom, He knows we were never meant to carry the weight of all His knowledge. We live in a corrupt and imperfect world where death is inevitable. But death wasn't part of the original plan. I think that's why it hurts so much, because we weren't supposed to feel the pain of that kind of separation. In pain we think we want answers and reasons, but what we really need is to know that there is hope somewhere, that this pain we feel won't hurt this bad forever, that somehow we will be able to survive.

In An Instant

In the months following bringing Sarah home from the hospital, I don't even know how to describe the daily emotional struggle. Only over the course of time would we know what or if there would be long-term effects from her prematurity and extended stay in the hospital. I wanted to just pretend that she was just like every other baby, and everything would be fine. I didn't have time to deal with the deep grief that I still felt because I was busy taking care of Sarah and displaying the role of the good pastor's wife. Then there was this secret inner struggle of questioning my whole worldview and everything I thought I knew about God being turned upside down. So much energy was put into appearing the way I thought everyone expected. It wasn't just a mask I put on every day; it was an entire costume. And it was exhausting.

Every Sunday and Wednesday, I walked through the doors of that little church, dressed up with a smile on my face, and holding Sarah close. The goal was to get to my seat for church to start with as little interaction as possible. I was there for everyone to see, but I wasn't there to spend time with God. I didn't want to talk about Him. I didn't want to pray or sing songs or listen to what the pastor had to say. I was content in my anger. I wanted to stay angry, because if I let it go, then I would in some way be saying that Alanna's death was okay and that I was moving on. I thought that meant that her memory had to stay in the past and that I wouldn't be allowed to hurt and ache for her anymore.

I'm not sure when it started but somehow, I knew it was the voice of God speaking to me in a small whisper. Ever so gently, He would say, *"Just let it go."* It never was a judgmental, harsh voice. It wasn't pushy or overwhelming. It was soft, subtle, and as far as I can remember, just once a day or one time each church service. I had fought to ignore it, to pretend like I didn't hear it so that I could remain mad at God, to hold on to my bitterness. Repeatedly, I would say in my heart, "No, I'm not letting this go." And I fought to stay angry.

But the thing about fighting is, eventually you get tired. I remember so vividly standing quietly during worship time in that little church as I had done for so long. I heard that little voice one more time. The slight nudge. The quiet voice whispered, *"Just let it go."* But this day was different. I was tired. I was tired of being mad. I was tired of holding it all in. I was tired of fighting, and I didn't want to be angry anymore.

There was a moment in the service that day, a call to come and spend time at the altar in God's presence. He gently whispered once again, *"Just let it go."*

For a moment, I struggled. How do I do this? How do I turn back to God after being so mad at Him for so long? How do I start a conversation with Him again? How will He react? Does He even want me back? I slowly lifted my hands in surrender, planning to have to explain myself, ready to plead my case to the Almighty Creator as if before a judge, and wondering how this forgiveness thing was really going to work.

But, before I could say a word, in an instant, the presence of the Holy Spirit came over me in the most powerful way, something I had never experienced so strongly in my life. There I stood, hands raised in surrender, trembling and weeping. It was as if I was physically wrapped in the arms of God Himself and nothing else mattered. After hearing about God for my first thirty years of life, *only then* did I finally understand who He really was. The moment I turned to Him for help, a wave of healing washed over me. The bitterness and anger melted away in an instant. I could *feel* the love of the Almighty God that day. I don't know how much time passed, but I went to my seat knowing that I had been in the presence of God.

I didn't fully understand it at the time, but looking back I realized that forgiveness, the way we understand it, is only a tiny fraction of what our Heavenly Father freely gives to us. His forgiveness was immediate and complete. In an instant, I was forgiven. In an instant, my Savior welcomed me back home, wrapped His arms around me, and reminded me of His unconditional love.

He took no time to think about whether to forgive me or not. He didn't weigh the pros and cons of offering me forgiveness. He didn't make me feel shame. There was no manipulation. He just loved me and wanted me back. And He was waiting right there, watching for me. God's forgiveness is not like ours. It is so much better. And for that, I am forever grateful.

I think about the parable of the lost son in Luke chapter fifteen. The son had demanded his inheritance and then turned his back on his father and walked away. He was no longer bound by his father's rules and was finally free to live life to the fullest. Eventually, the money ran out and the new friends were nowhere in sight. Desperate and hungry, he got a job feeding pigs but was so hungry himself that he began to crave their food.

In an instant, my Savior welcomed me back home, wrapped His arms around me and reminded me of His unconditional love.

But no one gave him anything. At this point he remembered that his father always provided plenty of food for his servants. The son began to plan. He would let his father know he had messed up, that he recognized he would never be part of the family, and then he would ask for a job. No doubt, on the long journey home he rehearsed and changed his speech many times to be sure he said the right things as he determined his father's different responses. But then, the unthought-of happened—a scenario totally unexpected to him. As he was still a long way off, the father saw him and was filled with compassion and ran to him. The servants were instructed to bring him a new robe, put a ring on his finger, and get him some sandals. Then they celebrated and ate together.

A robe: The father gave him a robe, which removed the evidence of his wild living and time in the pigpen.

A ring: The father placed a ring on his finger, which restored him to perfect sonship with authority.

Sandals: The sandals for his feet, which provided cleansing and care to heal the wounds from the journey and protection for his feet to go forward.

Celebration: The celebration, which gave him a place of honor at the table with an abundance of food.

Forgiveness, the way we tend to think of it is choosing not to be mad at the person who hurt you, or not holding it against them any longer.

The father could have had pity on the son as someone he once loved, and given him a plate of food to satisfy his most basic need—hunger. He could have tossed the son some scraps to fill his belly and sent him on his way.

But that is not how God's forgiveness works. He replaces the yucky stuff with a new robe of righteousness (Isaiah 61:10). He restores us, not to work off a debt as a slave but as his children (Galatians 4:4-7). He cleanses and wraps our wounds so healing can begin (Psalm 147:3). He reserves our seat at His table to be constantly filled and sustained as we fellowship with Him (Isaiah 46:4). God's forgiveness comes with full restoration and with gifts that are a sign that we belong to Him again.

* * *

Just like the son in the parable, I had my speech prepared. I was going to let God know I had messed up, and hopefully, He would tolerate me for a while until I could get it together and make better choices. At the bare minimum, the son was just hoping for some food. I just didn't want to be angry.

But, just like the father in the parable, God didn't let me finish presenting my case. I was the prodigal that day. And the Lord of all creation celebrated over me. He surrounded me with such a sweet spirit and softened my heart again. Ezekiel 11:19 (NLT) says, "I will give them an undivided heart and put a new spirit in them; I will remove from them their heart of stone and give them a heart of flesh. And I will give them singleness of heart and put a new spirit within them. I will take away their stony, stubborn heart and give them a tender, responsive heart, so they will obey my decrees and regulations. Then they will truly be my people, and I will be their God."

That day, my stubborn heart became soft again. I felt my heart of stone turn to flesh. Only then did healing begin. I opened my heart once again to the God I had known my whole life. The God I had shut out loved me enough to draw me back to Him. I had never known such a powerful and pivotal moment in all my life. My understanding of the God I had grown up hearing about suddenly shifted. He became personal.

There's a saying I've heard many times in church: "If you feel far from God, who moved?" We have this visual perception that when we turn our backs on God and walk away, we are putting distance between us and God, as if He were a person that we could physically move away from. We've all had close friends in our lives who have moved away, whether it be for a job or to go to college. There is physical distance that now separates what at one time would have been the best of friends. When you go from seeing someone daily to a phone call once a week, the relationship just isn't the same. Sure, you can plan a trip to spend a few days together, and, in some ways, it feels like you were never apart. But then you both go home, back to your regular lives, and wait for the next time to travel the distance to see each other. We assume that when we alienate ourselves from

God, that distance must be traveled again to get back to where we were.

What God showed me that day, and really what He had been trying to show me for months, was that He doesn't just stay put and let us walk away from Him. His love is not passive. He follows us, whatever the distance, gently whispering after us to just turn around.

That Was You

One day, when our son Micah was a little over a year old (Sarah would have been three at this time), he and Sarah were playing in the living room. A friend had come over that day to talk with me about some things she was struggling with in her life. As Micah ran across the hardwood floor, he fell, bumped his head, and began to cry. I hurried over, picked him up, and returned to the couch where I had been with my friend. We all know that mom kisses can heal boo-boos, so I hugged him, kissed his head, tried to calm and comfort him, but he kept pushing me away. After a few moments of this, realizing I wasn't making it any better, I thought, *All right, I'll just wait until he's done crying. Mom's kisses aren't working this time.*

In that moment, I heard the voice of God speak so clearly, saying, "That was you. You were hurting and I tried to comfort you, but you didn't want anything to do with me, so I let you just sit there on my lap and cry."

I'll never forget that moment. When I look back on my time of sorrow, the picture forever ingrained in my mind is sitting in the lap of an Almighty God. That first night of shock and piercing pain, the lonely days in a hospital room missing one baby and pleading for healing of the other, the nights crying myself to sleep—He was there. He wanted to comfort me. He wanted me to turn to Him so that He could be a Father to me. He was there. In the most miraculous way, He has traded my memories of loneliness with those of having a Heavenly Father right by my side.

There have been times since then when I have been crying, overwhelmed by a situation. I curl up in a chair and envision myself curled up like a small child sitting in her daddy's lap. The goodness of God I finally understood that day was that He allowed me the grace to grieve. He allowed me the time to sort through all the stuff I didn't know how to handle. He gave me the space I thought I wanted to sit and be angry about my pain. He didn't force me to find comfort in Him, but He sat, patiently waiting for His child to realize that all she had to do was lean in.

The goodness of God I finally understood that day was that He allowed me the grace to grieve.

I wish I had done things differently. If I could go back and change the way I dealt with my grief, I think the healing could have happened sooner. But I can't.

I put a lot of unspoken expectations on myself of how I could grieve, what I was allowed to tell whom, and how much I could let out. Even years later, I still feel the loss of our daughter. This tiny baby girl that lived only seventy-five hours outside of my womb still has an impact on our lives today. There are days I don't think about her as much, but then her name gently passes through my thoughts. Then there are days I just want to lay in bed and cry because my arms ache with the desire to give her a hug.

He knows, sees, and feels the pain we are experiencing. He watched me struggle through the overwhelming grief of this unimaginably tragic loss. And He wasn't offended. He didn't punish me for my lack of faith or my deliberate silence toward Him. His voice wasn't one of scorn or shame. He allowed me the grace to grieve.

Through all the stages of grief:

- Shock was met with grace—When I was in disbelief that God allowed this to happen. I immediately turned my back on Him, yet He remained faithful.
- Bargaining was met with grace—Through all my *Whys* and trying to find someone to blame. My questions never offended Him.

- Depression was met with grace—In my darkest times He held me even though I couldn't see it.
- Anger was met with grace—When I blamed Him and didn't want anything to do with Him, He let me be angry but never left me.
- Acceptance was met with grace—when I finally realized that He was my only hope, He lovingly welcomed me home.
- There is grace for the grieving.

I had always assumed my questions, doubts, struggling, and running from God would bring on His wrath. Each failure came with the fear of wondering when my punishment would come. However, that was not my experience. Instead, He met me with gentleness, kindness, forgiveness, and healing. The grace of God is so much more than a one-time gift at salvation as I thought. Grace is a gift given to us repeatedly. It is God's generous gift of favor that is abounding in love (Exodus 34:6), a sufficient source of strength (2 Corinthians 12:9), the essence of the very throne room of the Almighty (Hebrews 4:16).

You Are Good

There was a day about five or so years after the girls were born, that I remember sitting in the driveway of our house, allowing the song "You Are Good" by Kari Jobe to finish playing on the radio. The idea of calling God good hit me so hard that day. Is He really good? What is good? What does it mean to say God is good?

Good: to be morally excellent.[3]

Up until that point, I hadn't really understood what it meant to call God good.

Psalm 34:8 says, "O taste and see that the Lord is good" KJV.

Luke 18:18-19 tells this story of a young ruler who calls Jesus a Good Teacher, to which Jesus responds that only God is good.

"Good" is one of those words we throw around that can mean any number of things. We tell our kids to *be good* when we are leaving them in someone else's care, meaning that we want them to behave and use proper manners. After a meal, we can post reviews online about how good the food was (or wasn't). Sometimes we can watch a *good* movie or read a *good* book. But none of this seems to fit in with what Jesus is saying.

The word used here in the original Greek is *agathos*—good, perfect, complete, upright, kind, benevolent, useful, acceptable, wholesome, beneficial.[4] In all the places this word is found in the New Testament, not once is it talking about food or the manners of children. It's referring to: choosing to sit at Jesus' feet (Luke 10:42); genuine care for other people (Acts 9:36); the gospel message (Romans 10:15); God's perfect will (Romans 12:2); hope for eternity (2 Thessalonians 2:16); the way to overcome evil (Romans 12:21); the good works of laboring for God (Ephesians 2:10); a clear conscience (1 Peter 3:21).

Goodness can only originate in one place—within the construct of the Creator's design.

For the first time, I recognized that God was good. I could look back on those specific times, when He spoke, when He forgave, and when He called to me. It wasn't about doing good things for me. It was His abounding love, His *beautiful grace*, and unending *kindness* that drew me back to Him. I sang it and I meant it with everything in me. He's not just good when things go my way or when life is easy. His nature is good. His character is good. God *is* good. God's goodness isn't determined by the circumstances of life. Rather it is who He is.

What eventually became so apparent to me was that God treated me with kindness, which was the opposite of how I had assumed He would deal with me. No longer did the scripture passages of wrath and anger stand out, but it was:

- "I led Israel along with my ropes of kindness and love" Hosea 11:4 (NLT).
- "I have loved thee with an everlasting love: therefore with lovingkindness I have drawn thee" Jeremiah 31:3 (KJV).
- "Or do you have contempt for the wealth of his kindness, forbearance, and patience, and yet do not know that God's kindness leads you to repentance?" Romans 2:4 (NET).

I discovered for myself that God is good. That He still cared for me, even when I walked away from Him. He didn't come in and fix all the things I thought I needed Him to fix. He didn't come in as an angry tyrant, shaming me and putting me in my place. He came into my world and showed me that He not only saw me, but that He cared. God

> I discovered for myself that God is good…He came into my world and showed me that he not only saw me, but that He cared.

does not deal in shame. He calls to us, He *draws* us with kindness.

Since I know that God is good, then I can trust that no matter what happens to me, my family, my loved ones that He will take care of me. He was with me. His promise wasn't that He would keep bad things from happening to us. His promise is:

- "I will never leave thee or forsake thee" Hebrews 13:5 (KJV).
- "Peace I leave with you, my peace I give unto you..." John 14:27 (KJV).
- "My grace is sufficient for thee…" 2Corinthians 12:9 (KJV).

And he declares of himself:

- "The God of compassion and mercy! I am slow to anger and filled with unfailing love and faithfulness. I lavish unfailing love to a thousand generations. I forgive iniquity, rebellion and sin…" Exodus 34:6-7 (NLT).

God's message to us is that *regardless* of circumstances, we have help to get us through. The purpose of the Holy Spirit is to be our helper, our advocate, our strength, and we can't make it without Him.

If God doesn't take care of this the way I think He should, He is still good, and He is trustworthy. If I don't see justice in my lifetime, God is still good, and He is just. If my life isn't overflowing with abundant prosperity and riches, God is still good, and He is my provider. I will still believe that my God is good. Even in heartache, even in betrayal, even in the suffering that comes in this life. My God is good.

So, if God is good, then I can trust Him to be the one in control.

I Still Want To Be Your Father

At a women's conference in 2017, during a time of prayer and worship following the speaker's message, something she had said brought back a flood of memories from when Sarah was in the hospital and the first few years of her life. Suddenly, all the pain, all the struggles, the grieving, the desperate cries for God to heal her rushed back in and I became aware of the deep wounds still in my heart. I thought they were far behind me. This was nine years later, I should be better by now, right? I had already dealt with the loss and the struggle of my past. Everything is good now, right? I couldn't let hurt and grief pop back up. That would mean God wasn't enough.

Suddenly, I was completely aware of the pain I had tried to bury. In some ways, I still felt like I needed to show people that perfect image of a pastor's wife. John had accepted a position as Youth Pastor three years earlier at a different church, where most of the people didn't know our story. They knew of our miracle baby and a little of our loss, but not all the messy stuff. I didn't understand why this was happening, so I knelt at my seat, and I began to weep. Uncontrollable, heavy, deep weeping. I couldn't do or say anything or even pray.

The Lord gently pointed out to me that I had stopped praying for Sarah to continue to be healed. God had brought her through so much, but there were still some residual effects from being born so prematurely—muscle development issues and struggles with processing and remembering information, things that I was just hoping she would grow out of. All this time as I stood on the words the Lord had spoken to me, I was looking back. I remembered what I consider my *God moment* the day Micah fell and refused to be comforted. He had spoken to me saying, *That was you. You were hurting so I let you sit on my lap and cry.* Ever so gently, with that same sweet voice, He spoke again to me, saying, *I still want to be your Father.* I had failed to realize that the God who loved me through my circumstances in the past still wanted to love me and guide me and continue to heal Sarah's body. He wanted me to continue to sit on His lap as His child. It wasn't just a one-time event. I'm learning more and more how much of a constant presence God wants to have in the lives of His children.

As I sat back into my seat, I thanked the friend sitting next to me for praying for me as I had felt her hand on my shoulder. She said she could feel such an overwhelming sadness in me. The wounds of grief are deep and can remain hidden for a long time. By pushing the feelings down and pretending they aren't there won't make them disappear. They will eventually find their way to the surface. My grief wasn't completed just because time had passed. Those moments brought a cleansing and healing to my heart.

"Those who live in the shelter of the Most High will find rest in the shadow of the Almighty" Psalm 91:1 (NLT).

Throughout the Old Testament, as the prophets urged the people to turn from their wickedness, the pictures of death and destruction and judgment are so vivid and prevalent. Some days, reading the books of the prophets can be so heavy and hard to digest. But, as God's Word is becoming more familiar, I know a ray of hope is coming. At some point during the prophet's messages to the Israelites, there will be a shift from the impending doom to a message of hope. Jeremiah 31:33-34 (NLT) says:

> "But this is the new covenant I will make with the people of Israel on that day," says the Lord. "I will put my instructions deep within them, and I will write them on their hearts. I will be their God, and they will be my people. And they will not need to teach their neighbors, nor will they need to teach their relatives, saying, 'You should know the Lord.' For everyone, from the least to the greatest, will know me already," says

> the Lord. "And I will forgive their wickedness, and I will never again remember their sins."

In the book of Jeremiah, the prophet was tasked with a message: *Repent and turn to God, or you will be punished.*

I'll be honest, I used to see only God's anger. My view of Him, at least of who I thought He was, affected the way I read the Old Testament. I saw: the God of the Old Testament was angry and cruel, then Jesus came, and now He is full of grace. That is until I experienced the Father's kindness. Is God angry at the wickedness of the people? Absolutely! But that's not all. The covenant He made with the Israelites says: "And I will walk among you, and will be your God, and ye shall be my people" Leviticus 26:12 (KJV). He didn't just say it once, but He reminded them several times through the prophets in the Old Testament.

And every single time, it was about God calling the people to return to Him. This is not a God who is demanding and harsh and controlling. He knows their evil ways will only lead to destruction and death, yet He loves and desires to show kindness. It's His kindness and everlasting love that draws us to Him (Jeremiah 31:3, Hosea 11:4, Romans 2:4).

After spending time studying a particular passage, I came to love the book of Jeremiah. An encounter with God opened my eyes to see His love and compassion for His people. Even in their wickedness, He kept calling to them! Message after message throughout Jeremiah over the course of forty years. God had warned the Israelites, yet throughout it we hear:

- “Return...I will not be angry forever” Jeremiah 3:12 (NIV).
- “Return...for I am your husband. I will choose you” Jeremiah 3:14 (NIV).
- “How gladly would I treat you like sons” Jeremiah 3:19 (NIV).

God reminded them of the covenant He had made with the people long ago, saying:

“When I led your ancestors out of Egypt, it was not burnt offerings and sacrifices I wanted from them. This is what I told them: ‘Obey me, and I will be your God, and you will be my people. Do everything as I say, and all will be well!’” Jeremiah 7:22-23 (NLT).

The Bible is sometimes viewed as one big rule book, all the things we can and can’t do. It’s a bunch of rituals and sacrifices, and sometimes things that appear weird and don’t make any sense in our culture. But God established the rules to show us that He knows what’s best for us as we obey and follow Him as our guide.

The heart of God is one of mercy ready to be poured out. He calls, He watches, He waits for us. But the most incredible part of all is that He wants us to walk with Him. The messages are: come to Me, I will dwell among you, I will walk with you, I will transform your broken and sinful heart and give you My spirit so that you will know Me.

As a mom, especially when our children are young, our attention is pulled from the moment we wake—who am I kidding! Even when we are sleeping sometimes!—in so many different directions: taking care of the kids, cleaning the house, cooking breakfast, lunch, and dinner, trying to fit in fun activities and play dates, keeping the sports schedule, getting everyone dressed and ready for church, finishing homework. And sometimes... we feel like we must carry it all, do it all with a smile, and keep everyone happy without getting frustrated. After all, this is the life I wanted. And we forget. No matter what our life circumstances have brought, no matter the good or bad, God says, "I'm your Father. Let's walk through this together. Yes, we made it through that last struggle. I'm still here. Yes, life is good right now so let's continue to do it together."

> I'm your Father. Let's walk through this together...

My Father...

When I think about God as "my Father" I immediately think about the Lord's prayer that begins:

"Our Father ... "

God is referred to as "the God of Abraham" or "the God of your fathers" in the Old Testament as a way of distinguishing Him from other pagan gods. As children, we are taught to believe what our parents believe. Growing up in the church, I was raised to believe in and follow the God of my parents, David and Brenda, or the God of my grandparents, Lester and Lola. I believed what they taught me, and I took their word for it. I think to some degree, even into my twenties, I still viewed Him as the God of my parents, the God I was supposed to have faith in and trust in simply because that's what I was taught. I was so blessed to have wonderful parents who were honest, hardworking, faithful, and committed to raising their kids in church. But when something happens that shakes you to the core and causes your world to be turned upside down, holding on to the faith of someone else isn't enough. My parents' faith in God didn't help me feel better, and it certainly didn't heal my broken heart.

The healing came when God became *my Father.* When I knew Him as the one who held me on His lap, like a child, and let me cry. When I knew Him as the Father who just wanted His daughter to come back home.

Response To Tough Times

Growing up in a Christian family, church was life. There was never a question of whether we would go to church. We were there for it all. Sunday morning service, Sunday school, Sunday evening service, and Wednesday night classes. From the time I was five when we moved from the Pentecostal Church of God to First Assembly of God in Jefferson City, we were members of that church until we moved for John to attend Bible college. My dad's whole family attended, and my uncle was, and still is, the pastor.

I still remember the first time I began to question God and what I truly believed about Him. When I was in junior high, one of my other uncles and aunt divorced. As I watched the pain it caused my cousins and how it changed our family, I would lie in bed and cry out to God on their behalf. I realized then that as I was desperate for God to answer me, there seemed to be silence. It felt like my prayers would leave my lips, float upward, and stop at my bedroom ceiling and go no further. While I prayed and talked to God, I never really waited for an answer, nor did I expect one. I always thought the idea of God talking directly to people was reserved for the super spiritual, or at least someone more spiritual than I was. I expected that if God were to speak personally to me, it would be some big booming voice chastising me for being selfish, or that God was somewhat annoyed by me now, so the answer was "No." I had assumed that prayer, for the most part, was one-sided. We are supposed to pray over our food, talk to Him about the struggles and bad things happening in our lives and then wait to see if He does anything about it.

I unintentionally developed a response to tough times. I would pray for a person or situation and then wait and hope that everything would turn out okay. If it didn't, I would kind of be mad at God for a little while and then move on. This ended up becoming the cycle of my relationship to God.

The first time I experienced God talking to me was one Wednesday night in the youth service when I was about seventeen. I had been feeling like I just wasn't good enough, like I couldn't do anything right. As the service neared its end, I knelt at the altar and cried to God about all my failures. Somewhere, in the middle of it all, I prayed, "God, I just want to know that You are pleased with me." It wasn't something I normally prayed for, but the words were specific. As I sat there at the altar a little longer, a close friend of mine came to me and said, "I feel like God wants me to tell you that He is pleased with you." Now, any skeptic could come along and say, "People go around encouraging each other all the time. This could have just been a friend who saw you crying and wanted to make you feel better." But I can say, I had never before said to God that "I want to know that you are pleased with me." I was shocked and humbled that God would speak to me through my friend.

As I have grown and become more familiar with God's voice and how He speaks to His children, I've often wondered if He didn't try to tell me that Himself and I just didn't hear it, or assumed it was just my own thoughts. Yet, in His kindness and patience, He spoke to me in a different way.

It was the endless cycle of praising God in the good times, then blaming Him for the bad that resulted in my complete turning of my back on Him after the death of our little girl. While I knew a lot about Him and all the things He had done, I didn't understand Him, and I never really trusted Him. I mean, I thought I did, but I didn't. While I hoped He would answer my prayers, I wasn't ever really sure. My trust in Him was very superficial. Then, after Alanna's death, I didn't trust Him at all. Since He didn't save one of our babies, I couldn't really trust Him with the other. My prayers turned into just hoping that Sarah would be okay. I knew word had traveled fast, and thousands of people across the country were praying for her. In a way I figured that there was a better chance that God would answer all of their prayers over mine.

I didn't realize that this idea of not trusting God with my children had carried forward. I thought I had made amends, come to understand God in a much deeper way, and my relationship with Him had been fully reconciled. That is until Joshua became sick.

In June of 2019, when he was seven years old, Joshua, our youngest, began complaining that his stomach was hurting. It was the week of soccer camp at our church—something fun that he had been looking forward to. Each night as we prepared to leave the house, he cried, begging to stay home. He was in constant pain and felt sick to his stomach. This went on for two months before we were able to get him to a GI specialist. He had blood tests and an ultrasound. We eliminated dairy and gluten from his diet. Every test that was run came back normal. One day while I was praying for him, I ended by telling God that I trusted Him. Almost immediately there was a twinge in my heart and a question came to my mind, *Do you? Do you really trust Me?*

Honestly, I don't know if I ever really did. I just always assumed that everything was going to be okay. But did I trust Him with my kids? For a time, the answer was a resounding, "NO!" No, I didn't trust Him. After all, He had let me down in a pretty big way. How could I trust Him? After all this time, did I still not trust Him? To be perfectly honest, I hadn't really thought about it. Trust is not one of those things that you automatically give to another person. Over time, people will prove to you whether they are trustworthy or not. We learn who we can trust with a secret, which friend we can depend on in a crisis, and who to call when we are feeling down and just know they will encourage us or make us laugh. When we trust someone, we give them a piece of us, a little bit of our heart or our well-being. So, when trust is broken, that piece of us hurts and the relationship with that person is damaged. We learn how to protect ourselves from people so they can't hurt us again.

As I wrestled with the question: *Do I really trust God?* I made the decision—more of a resolve—that *Yes, with intention, God, I do trust you.* We never got any answers, and Josh continued to deal with the pain on and off, but eventually it went away. My trust in the faithful God, however, has continued to grow.

The God Who Sees Me

There is a woman in the book of Genesis named Hagar, an Egyptian slave. She's not a well-known character in the Bible, but her story is significant. Abram and Sarai—before their names were changed to Abraham and Sarah—were waiting on God's promise to be fulfilled. The Lord had revealed to Abram that he would be the father of many nations, that his offspring would outnumber the stars in the heavens or the dust of the earth.

As they grew older and the chances of this promise being fulfilled lessened, they decided to take matters into their own hands. Sarai chose to give her Egyptian slave to Abram as his wife to have a child. This was a common practice at the time because barren women were often shamed. Children born to the slave were then considered the children of the wife. While this was culturally acceptable, it wasn't God-ordained or approved. When Hagar became pregnant, naturally, conflict arose between Sarai and Hagar. It was a direct result of Sarai's actions, and the outcome was what she had originally wanted. However, she eventually realized this was not the fulfillment of God's promise she had hoped for, rather the disappointing substitute left her feeling jealous and bitter. When she brought the matter to her husband, he told her to do what she thought best. Sarai treated Hagar so harshly that she chose to run away (Genesis 16:1-6).

It is natural to feel abandoned when the unfairness of life happens, especially when it is something out of our control due to the consequence of someone else's bad choices.

As Hagar rested near a spring in the desert, the angel of the Lord found her. He called her by name and even mentioned her position as Sarai's servant. He already knew of her situation but still chose to ask her about what was going on so that she could share her sorrow. She is then directed to give the baby the name Ishmael, which means "God hears" because the Lord had heard her cries for help. "Thereafter, Hagar used another name to refer to the Lord, who had spoken to her. She said, 'You are the God who sees me.' She also said, 'Have I truly seen the One who sees me?'" (Genesis 16:13 NLT).

This brief conversation tells us so much about God's character. He knows who we are, what we do, and where we go. He knows what is happening in our lives yet cares enough to listen to us tell our side of the story. He comes to us. He sees. He hears.

* * *

When darkness surrounds us, the automatic assumption is that God does not see, or He does not care about us. I had concluded that I must have done something that caused God to no longer want to answer my prayers. If I needed prayer, I depended on someone else praying because it was more likely that He would answer their prayer instead of mine. God saw Hagar where she was and cared for her. It was not by accident that the angel of the Lord came across Hagar in the desert. He did not have to go on a journey to search her out. He knew exactly where she was because the Lord had been watching her the whole time.

> He comes to us. He sees. He hears.

In my own dark times, God never showed up visibly in any form. I never heard Him speak to me in an audible voice. And at the time, I convinced myself that He did not care. Only by looking back can I remember the sweetness of His small voice calling to me. From that moment on, I have heard His voice hundreds of times, calling to me, leading me, answering me. And I too can declare, "You are the God who sees me. . . You have heard my prayers." I am humbled, and many times it brings me to my knees as I realize the God of all creation—the God who loved me when I despised Him, the God who called to me when I pretended not to or refused to hear, the God who was always faithful when I was far from it—sees me.

In 2021, John resigned from the church where he had been the Youth Pastor for seven years. We had no specific direction, only that God had said that He would lead us to a place we do not yet know.

That first visit to a new church was hard, hard on the whole family. The drive to church was emotional, and I think we all felt a little lost. Micah just wanted to watch church online. Sarah didn't go to the youth service, and chose to stay with us in the adult prayer service. I'm pretty sure I cried throughout the entire message. As the service was wrapping up, the pastor directed everyone to get into small groups for prayer, as was their usual practice on Wednesday evening. We sat there for a moment looking at each other, not sure if we should find someone to pray with or if people would come to us. After a brief, awkward moment a young lady that had been on the opposite side of our row came and sat in front of us. We quickly exchanged names, and she asked if we had any prayer requests. John gave a very short answer about being a pastor waiting on the Lord to lead us into our next ministry position. She said, "That's interesting, because from the moment I sat down and saw you, I just kept hearing *Pastor, he's a pastor.* in my spirit." As she prayed, the power and presence of the Holy Spirit was evident, and she said she could feel the anointing of God on our lives.

When we got home, I couldn't help but wonder, *Why did God do that? Why did He tell her John was a pastor? Why did He let her, a stranger, know about an anointing on our lives?* We kind of just wanted to go to a big church to be invisible. As I questioned this, even into the next day, the Lord gently reminded me of Hagar's story. It was His way of saying, *I still see you. You are still who I have created you to be.* Even when we want to blend in or not be noticed by people, we have a Heavenly Father whose gaze we cannot escape.

There Was This Song...

When my husband and I were dating, he introduced me to a beautiful song about heaven called "Somewhere Beyond the Moon" by Michael O'Brien. It's about the heavenly place that God has prepared for those that believe and choose to follow Jesus. From the moment I heard it, I determined that it would be a lullaby for our babies someday. I had this perfect picture in my mind of what motherhood would look like. I would sit in a rocking chair, gently kiss my babies on the forehead, and sing softly to them as they fell asleep.

I was never able to sing the song as a lullaby for Sarah. I tried every now and then but could barely make out the first couple of lines before breaking down. It was years before I could finally sing it to our youngest. It became a song that John sang to them often as they were growing. Initially, we thought it would be such a purposeful way to gently teach our kids about heaven. But the thought of our little girl in heaven was just too difficult for me to celebrate for a while because this wasn't the way it was supposed to be. This song actually turned into something so much more significant than I ever could have imagined.

We never wanted our kids to *just find out* someday that they had a sister. We have a couple of pictures in our house of Alanna, and we talk about her often. Our children go through the grieving process as they understand more and more the emptiness left by her life. We get to remember Alanna and think about what she might look like and what she is doing in heaven. Heaven becomes a little more real and tangible, instead of some imaginary dreamland.

While we are still living on this earth, we can only imagine the beauty our eyes will behold when we pass from this life to the next. But I know the very first thing our baby girl saw when she finally was able to open her eyes was the face of Jesus. Knowing Alanna is in the care of the Creator of the universe, the only one who could love her more than us, is a comfort to this mama's heart. Usually, on the anniversary of her passing, and in other moments when I'm just thinking about her, I'll ask Jesus to give my girl a hug for me. Moments when my arms ache to hold her but can't, I know He will.

Living with Grief

Our first holiday after bringing Sarah home, we spent in Springfield at John's uncle and aunt's house. It was a joy to be able to share our daughter with family and celebrate Thanksgiving together.

That afternoon, as I stared out the window and rocked my sweet girl to sleep for nap time, would be the first of many celebrations where I was grateful for time to be away from everyone else to grieve the loss of our Alanna. Christmas, birthdays, vacations, big holidays to special family dinners, the emptiness felt by her absence would pierce my heart. But as the years pass, some of those occasions provide memory without pain. I have often felt guilty for not thinking about her when *I think I should have*. How could I forget about her? After a loss, it is easy to fall into a trap of following some theoretical nonexistent timeline of expectations for recovery at a pace set by others or even more so of those pesky *unspoken* rules we place on ourselves.

A few years ago, I had been so busy planning Sarah's birthday party that I didn't even think about Alanna until a few days later, on the anniversary of the day she died. I often pray on her birthday for Jesus to give her a big hug from me, and I felt so horrible that I forgot. I still love her, and she will always be part of our family. Somewhere along the way, though, as I journeyed through grief, healing began to take place. But it doesn't just happen on its own. It is a process that takes time, walking through pain *with* the Father, the only one who can heal the brokenhearted (Psalms 147:3).

Our Princess of Victory (the meaning of Sarah Nicole)

Earlier in our story, I mentioned that it was discovered that Sarah needed to have a PDA ligation, a minor surgery to close a vein in her heart. Typically, this vein closes at birth, but hers remained open. At the time, the procedure was successful, but it wasn't until two months later that we discovered that something had happened during surgery.

After two-and-half months of needing so much support to breathe, we rejoiced the day Sarah was finally able to breathe mostly on her own. After being intubated, then using a CPAP, she graduated to only needing a nasal canula. It was a day of celebration, and the NICU staff made sure we were going to be there when the tape was removed that held everything in place and the bulky contraption was removed from her face. We had not ever been able to see her whole face. John briefly saw her when she was born, but she was immediately intubated at that time.

After a couple days, I realized I had never heard her cry. She didn't make much sound at all. She had never been able to before, so I hadn't thought about it, but now she should be making some sound. It seems rather absurd to not hear your baby cry for the first two-and-half months of her life, but everything about the first two-and-half months was unusual. When I pointed this out to the doctor, he decided to do x-rays to see if something was wrong. It was discovered that during her PDA ligation, when she was two weeks old, the nerve to one of her vocal cords had been damaged. This was crucial at the time because she had been having problems eating and was constantly choking, and we didn't understand why. When a vocal cord is paralyzed, it causes difficulty swallowing, allowing food or liquids to slip into the lungs. We were told if the nerve was severed completely, there was nothing they could do about it, but if it was just damaged, there was a slight possibility it may heal. Either way, only time would tell how much this would affect her. One thing was for certain, the doctor said, "She will never be able to sing." We were both crushed. Singing has always been a passion and joy to us, and the thought of never hearing our daughter sing was devastating.

Sarah was also diagnosed with chronic lung disease. This happens when long-term use of a breathing machine injures a premature baby's lungs. In other words, one thing she needed to survive had also caused damage to her fragile and underdeveloped lungs. Again, the doctor was very clear, she would not be able to play sports or run and play for long periods of time. She most likely would wear out quickly and need to sit down often.

Due to the brain bleed sustained early on, there was a portion of her brain that was damaged. Only time would tell what exactly would be affected by this injury.

Retinopathy of prematurity was another condition that began to develop that brought a new fear, as it threatened her eyesight. The blood vessels of the retina were not completely developed. Since they were very fragile, the vessels have the potential of growing abnormally. The doctor came in to check her eyes often as the condition worsened. Stage 1 being the least severe up to Stage 5 leading to blindness. For Sarah, the condition advanced to Stage 4, which is defined as partial retinal detachment, which most likely would affect her vision. After a couple of weeks monitoring this, the ROP slowly improved. Later, she developed strabismus—a wandering eye—which at eighteen months required surgery to correct, along with therapy, the use of glasses, and an eye patch. She was a pretty cute little pirate, if I do say so myself. Although, trying to keep glasses or an eye patch on a strong-willed eighteen-month-old is not for the faint of heart!

Physical and occupational therapy were needed for her first years at home to help us work through a lot of the residual effects of being born so early. It wasn't until she was almost two that she was finally able to walk.

Eating solid food was quite a challenge. Because of being intubated for so long, she developed a texture aversion and ate only baby food and yogurt until she was three. This miracle came out of the blue, as it was something I had specifically asked God to heal her of only a week or two before. We were challenged at our church through a series on giving, to ask and believe God for miracles and for blessings as we were faithful to give. The day we wrote a check to give to the building project, I asked God to help our daughter to eat real food. Sidenote—giving to a church did not heal our daughter, we did not pay for a miracle, and writing a check did not require God to do something for us. I believe that God loves to answer prayers, and He chose to do this miracle for us at that time.

Malachi 3:10 says, "'Bring the whole tithe into the storehouse, that there may be food in my house. Test me in this,' says the Lord Almighty, 'and see if I will not throw open the floodgates of heaven and pour out so much blessing that there will not be room enough to store it.'"

I had made spaghetti and was feeding it to Micah, who was about a year and a half at this time. I thought, *Well, let's just see what Sarah does with this.* I gave her a plate of spaghetti, assuming she would play with it and probably make a mess. I was focused on feeding Micah, but after just a few minutes I turned around to check on Sarah. She had gobbled down the entire plateful and was just sitting in her chair with the biggest, messiest grin on her sauce-covered face! I sat there in shock for a bit before saying a prayer of thanksgiving to God for healing Sarah that day.

Every couple of years, Washington University asks for Sarah to come back for a follow-up of the brain and development study she was a part of there while in the NICU. They play with her, watch her do puzzles, and observe her development. They were always very kind to us, so we didn't mind going, and we were happy to continue to help with their research. Her ten-year checkup included an MRI of her brain. I always wondered about the area of her brain that had been injured due to the brain bleed when she was just a few days old. In the back of my mind, I was afraid that someday we would discover how that damaged area would affect her. About a month later, I realized they hadn't called back with the results, so I decided to call the office. The young lady who answered was a little confused. I said, "When she was a baby, she had a brain bleed that caused some damage, and I was just curious what they thought about it." She responded, "Usually they call the parents to give an update but let me check." After a brief hold, she came back on the line, "They didn't find anything in the scan. There is no damage. If there was anything irregular at all, they would have made a note about it, but there is nothing."

So many prayers had gone up on Sarah's behalf. So many nights of pleading for God to heal her, and He had answered, and we didn't even know it. It makes me wonder how many other problems, sicknesses, irregularities did she have that we never knew about that God healed in her tiny body.

I also want to point out that our daughter has never once had shortness of breath while playing, and actually could play longer and harder than all the other kids around her. She had more energy than I could keep up with most days! We've never had her lungs reexamined, but I don't feel the need, as there has never been one instance that her breathing was abnormal.

As for her vocal cord injury, Sarah did have difficulty for a while taking a bottle. She would get choked up at times, and would eat very slowly. We always made sure to feed her in the kitchen, away from couches and carpet, because if she spit up, it was an eruption. Yet, over time, her eating improved and she no longer had any issues, as far as we knew. There was still a flutter in her voice, usually only when she's a little sad or nervous about something or if she's trying to talk loudly. If you've been around her much, you can recognize it. After years of wondering, we finally made an appointment to know for sure what happened with her vocal cord, in the summer of 2023. A quick scope revealed that her left vocal cord was paralyzed. We followed up with a vocal therapist who gave her some vocal exercises that can help make her voice stronger. In noisy places, it can be difficult to hear her, but she is content with her soft-spoken nature. And, she has the most beautiful, soft singing voice you've ever heard! She's like a sweet little songbird.

On November 14, 2023, Sarah and I were reviewing her Hebrew homework, which was a study on the names of God. As we came to Yahweh Rapha, the God who heals, we talked about the story in Exodus 15, where the Lord had Moses throw a piece of wood into bitter water and the water became good to drink for a desperately thirsty nation. The Lord declares of himself "…for I am the Lord that healeth thee" (Exodus 15:26 KJV).

"Sarah, have you ever thought about asking God to heal your vocal cord?"

She shrugged, "No, not really."

"Do you want me to pray for you now? Would you mind if I anoint you with oil and pray for you?"

"Sure, you can."

I explained how oil is a representation of the Holy Spirit and James 5:14 instructs us to anoint the sick with oil in the name of the Lord and then I prayed: "Heavenly Father, thank You that You are the same today as You were thousands of years ago. You are a God who keeps His promises, and You are still Yahweh Rapha. You are a miracle worker, and I believe You can do a miracle now by healing Sarah's vocal cord. Thank You for hearing our prayers. We love You. In Jesus name, Amen."

I looked up at her and said, "Sometimes God heals instantly, sometimes it takes time, and sometimes we must ask over and over again. Let's have wild faith to believe that you are going to be healed."

We hugged, and I moved on with my day of errands. When I got back home, with a funny look on her face, she asked to speak to me alone.

"Mom, almost immediately after you prayed for me my neck felt different and I could feel vibrations. I've never felt anything on the left side of my neck before, but I can't stop touching it. I can feel that it's working now. When I swallow, everything is easier. Sometimes, while swallowing, I have to kind of swallow twice to get it all down, but now it's so much easier, and my throat feels more open. And I can yell because I was yelling at Josh to get out of my room, and I scared myself because I've never yelled that loud before. Oh, and the trill that's always been in my voice, I don't hear it anymore."

As she and the boys were talking and playing a game, I looked at John.

"I think I can hear the difference in her voice, can you?"

"Yes, she definitely sounds louder."

I had never realized the difficulty she still was having. I just assumed that she adapted to make do, but the difficulty was all she had ever known. She probably got tired of all my questions, but I couldn't help myself. I wanted to hear her yell and sing and talk. Her voice is so much clearer and stronger. I couldn't stop looking at her and smiling in amazement. God had healed her instantly while we sat at our kitchen table. What an awesome miracle-working God!

A few days later as I continued to thank God and pray over her, the gentle voice of the Father spoke again: *I'm not finished with her yet.* I see more miracles to come in her future. We will just have to wait to see.

Beautiful Grace

Living in grief is painful. There were days I felt so empty. Days I didn't want to get out of bed. Days when I wondered if it would ever get easier, if I could ever move on, if I could ever be happy again. Will it hurt this much for the rest of my life? I don't know if I can go on for a lifetime of *this*.

Families who may have these same questions swirling through your minds, if I could just let you know this: I have come to know a *beautiful grace* I would have never found under any other circumstances. Now, if I could go back and change what happened, I absolutely would, but I can't.

I thought I would always look back and only see my grief, only the sadness, only the desperation and hopelessness and emptiness, but that's not what I see anymore. My story on my own ended in darkness and separation. Yes, I remember those feelings, but do you know what covers my story? It's the *grace* of an Almighty God. It's the picture of Him holding me. It's knowing that the

God of the universe saw me in my pain rejecting Him, yet He loved me enough to just let me sit on His lap and cry. Sometimes He gave me what I thought I wanted—some space to figure out and do things on my own—without actually leaving me. My story on my own ended in darkness. But He took it over. His love overshadows it all. He brought hope again, He brought light again, He brought joy again. Until recently, I thought I was the main character in my story.

My husband and I enjoy watching home renovation shows. It amazes me to watch investors who have the vision to take an old, outdated, sometimes really messed-up house and make it beautiful and valuable again. From new tile in the bathroom and backsplashes in the kitchen to knocking down entire walls, homes are given new life. The most satisfying part is the transformation in the before and after pictures.

Look at this. This is how the house used to look with its dingy, small kitchen. We took out a wall to open it all up. Now the whole space is bright and clean with brand-new appliances and white cabinets. We refinished the bathrooms by putting in new plumbing because the old pipes were leaking. Now there's a beautifully tiled, walk-in shower where there once was a rusty old tub. There's new flooring and fresh paint, and the house looks brand-new. Then a staging crew comes in and adds furniture and décor to help potential buyers envision what the home could look like with all their own stuff in place.

Sometimes, I fall asleep and miss the second half of a show. The next day, when I realize it, I don't always go back and watch the demolition part. I'm just interested in the before and after pictures. The in-between work is hard and messy and challenging. There can be arguments about design and things not working out like they originally thought, or an underlying issue with the foundation that they didn't see in the initial walk-through before purchasing the home. The renovation ends up costing way more than the original estimate, and it always takes longer than they thought it would.

We tend to think of ourselves as the investor, as the one who must take our lives from the original structure, clean everything up, put in all the new stuff, and stage it so when people come for the open house we can show them how we've changed everything and made it new and pretty and better.

I am not the investor in this story. God is the one who saw this broken-down mess. He negotiated the price for me when Jesus laid down his life, not to cover the sin and ugliness like a fresh coat of paint, but to rewire and rebuild into something new and clean. Sometimes, load-bearing walls need to be taken down and support beams have to be added. Sometimes the cracks in the foundation need to be fixed. My flaws of doubt and unfaithfulness weren't brought to light so that I could work to make myself presentable. There was someone behind the scenes working through all the hard, messy stuff, exposing the corrosion, the problems underneath that I didn't realize were there. We want quick and easy before and after pictures. We want a smooth transition. We don't want the renovation to take too long.

But the One who knows us best, the One who can see deep down into the smallest details of every fiber of our being, wants to transform our understanding of who He is.

Boy, if I could go back and somehow keep this awful tragedy from happening, I would! What I wouldn't do to be given the chance to hold my baby girl, to raise her, to see what she would look like now!

But...

Because of this difficulty, I have met my Savior, and He is good. I can honestly say that I have come to know my Heavenly Father in a way that would not have been possible any other way.

When I set out to write this book, the idea was that if my story can help someone else know that they are not alone in their pain or struggle or doubt, then that's good enough for me. But my story doesn't give hope. All the things I did on my own can't bring peace or heal a broken heart or fill the void left behind after someone you love is gone. I can bring awareness, but I cannot work miracles. What I can do is point you to the only One who can. The main character in my story isn't me or Sarah. I thought we were. There was a loving Heavenly Father who was gently holding us, working one small miracle at a time just so that I could look back and see His hands in *everything*. So now this is His story. It's not about me. It's about Him. His involvement is evident throughout every story, every tear, every moment. He was working, even though I didn't always see it or feel it.

There was a loving Heavenly Father who was gently holding us, working one small miracle at a time just so that I could look back and see His hands in *everything*.

God is love. God is faithful. God is merciful.

And His *beautiful grace,* this unmerited favor that only He can offer, has nothing to do with me, or how good I try to be or anything I could ever do to repay Him. It is all about Him.

So, while I can tell of what I've experienced, what I've seen, what I've felt or known, it is only because of a God so good that I have hope.

The Things People Say (What to Do/Not to Do)

We were so thankful to be surrounded by people who loved us and cared for us during such a difficult time in our lives. Friends and family sent us gas cards, restaurant gift certificates, and all kinds of gift cards to help with the expenses of constantly driving back and forth to the hospital. People left meals at the church for John to bring home on the nights we were there, and some even brought meals to us at the hospital. We would get to introduce our tiny girl to them for the first time through the glass of the Isolette. We received so many cards with words of love, encouragement, and prayers. These are the things I remember fondly as I look back and recognize God's love poured out through His children.

Most people don't know what to do when a friend is grieving the loss of a loved one. John and I always joked that someday, if I ever write a book, it will include a chapter about the inconsiderate things people say or what not to say to hurting/grieving people. So here we go!

Let's start with **Common quote #1**: said to us and to probably every other person who has lost a loved one: *Everything happens for a reason.*

Nope, no, no it doesn't. This statement is not true at all. And it certainly was not helpful on the day we were burying our child. And if you are wondering, yes, I do remember who said it and where we were standing in the graveyard. I smiled and nodded with tears rolling down my cheeks, but those words pierced like a dagger. What reason could there possibly be that would make this okay? Do you know the reason? I don't know the reason. God didn't tell me in the thousand times I asked between the time she died and the day of the funeral.

I wanted a reason to help us grasp and make sense of this horror. It seems like if we can somehow make sense of it all, we could feel better or have some closure. We are desperate for someone to answer our whys and what-ifs. But the truth of it is that everything doesn't happen for a reason. If everything happens for a reason, the only reason is that life is unfair and imperfect. The world is evil, people make mistakes, and sometimes things just happen and we can't do anything about it.

When I was confronted with the question, I think it was the Lord who asked me, *If you knew the answer, would it make you feel better? No. Of course not.* Knowing the answer won't change the reality. And while I came to this conclusion that all the whys will never be answered, it doesn't just magically make everything okay.

I think Christians can distort the meaning of Romans 8:28 (NET) that says, *"And we know that all things work together for good for those who love God."* This doesn't mean that God causes all things to happen, whether good or bad. But that *when* things happen, He can still work it out and use it for His glory. In our situation, God didn't take our daughter so that I would have a reason to write a book. There have been good things that have come out of our loss, like the deeper understanding of God and an empathy to care for and pray for friends who have also experienced loss. God has given us dreams and ideas for future ways to help those dealing with loss that we probably wouldn't understand if we hadn't experienced it ourselves. Does that mean that God took Alanna so that we could experience the pain of losing a child to make a better impact on others? Absolutely not! But, since it happened, the trajectory of our lives has shifted into a new future plan where we get to share God's healing power and His constant love and care for us through pain.

Common quote #2: *At least you still have one.* Yes, this was said to me a few times by friends and acquaintances in the hospital.

We were extremely excited to be having twins. Two separate babies. After what seemed like a late start on growing our family, having twins was a great way to catch up. I knew it would be difficult, but I was really looking forward to it. No expectant mom goes into the hospital hoping for at least one of the two to make it. I loved two babies growing inside my womb. One surviving twin does not cancel out the grief of losing the other twin. Yes, I am grateful that I didn't lose both, but I gave birth to two separate babies, and only one got to come home. I have learned over time that a surviving twin feels the loss differently than everyone else. Because we never wanted our kids to discover they had a sister they didn't know about, and because I truly believe healing comes in talking about your tragedy/loss, we have been very open with our kids about Alanna.

As Micah, our middle child, is getting older, he at times will be very sad and say he misses Alanna and wishes she could be here. He was born almost two years later, and Josh four years later. They feel the emptiness of the space she left behind. But it's very different for Sarah. She has felt the loss and talks about it often. As she was approaching her twelfth birthday, she began asking really hard questions like, *Why did Alanna have to die but not me? I wish I could be in heaven with her. I don't want to wait till I die to see her, I want to know what she looks like now and play with her.* I wrestled with these same questions and had to come to terms with not ever knowing the answer to them. I am confronted with it all over again as my daughter asks me questions that I can't answer.

Every holiday, birthday, celebration, achievement for Sarah is mixed with the emptiness of another child that we don't get to celebrate. We aren't "lucky" that one survived. We still lost.

I would like to add to the list of what not to say by including *At least...* followed by anything else you can imagine. We have never experienced loss through miscarriage, but many people do. Women have talked to me about their miscarriages and will often compare it to my loss, in an attempt to diminish their pain or situation as not being as bad as mine. I've heard said about miscarriage things like:

- At least you weren't that far along.
- At least you still have your other children.
- At least you are young enough to try again.
- At least ______. Well, I'm sure you can fill in the blank.

These kinds of statements rob women and families of their ability to recognize and work through grief. No matter the stage of development of a baby, inside or outside of the womb, the hopes and dreams for that little one has already taken root in the hearts of the mom and dad. Not only are they grieving the death of their baby, but the dreams for the future with him or her has been stolen from them. These kinds of *at least* statements are detrimental to the healing process. They cause a constant feeling of *what's wrong with me?* or *Why can't I just get over this and move on?*

Silence is awkward. People don't know what to do. They want to say something helpful, something profound. Often, the words themselves offer no comfort at all. The outpouring of love we received during our time in the hospital was truly amazing. Gifts and meals were such a blessing! But, oh, how I dreaded having to talk to people. Hugs are great; I've always been a hugger. But I was on the verge of crying nearly every day. Some days I did want someone to talk to, but I wanted to do it on my terms in my time. If I was with other people, a distraction from the nightmare I was living was welcome. My mood shifted hourly sometimes depending on what news I was receiving that day.

Common quote #3: *Heaven gained another angel, or God needed another angel.*

Not only is this idea completely unbiblical, but the very thought of God taking our baby because he needed an angel brings no comfort whatsoever and attributes a cruel nature to God. To believe that He would give a precious gift of life to a family just to take it back is almost just as horrible as the loss itself. Angels exist because God created them as angels in the first place. For some, the idea that a loved one who has passed is looking down on us from heaven, watching over us, or becoming a guardian angel may help them feel like the person is still close by; however, this is not biblical and gives an incorrect picture of God's character and design.

During my time in ministry, I have encountered many people who are grieving after losing a loved one. I never say much. If there's any talking, it's the one who is grieving doing most of it, with me listening, caring, and crying with them. Grief on its own is painful, paralyzing, and debilitating. What I don't want at some point down the road is a grieving person replaying harmful untruths or clichés that I could have said to them just so I don't have to feel awkward in silent moments or to make myself sound extra spiritual. A hundred people could have been kind and spoken comforting words to us, but the ones we remember are these. Never during the grieving process has a friend asked me for advice on how to stop being so sad or how to not think about their loved one so much. They have, however, mentioned the comments other people have made to them:

- You need to just move on.
- It's been long enough.
- You need to get over it/you'll get over it.
- You'll get pregnant again.

(Insert the thought that came to your mind as you were reading this list)

If you are someone who tends to say phrases like this to a person who is grieving, let me just say: ***STOP IT!***

> If you are someone who tends to say phrases like this to a person who is grieving, let me just say: *STOP IT!*

No one can tell you when your grieving process is over; no one can tell you how much time is enough. Grief is not the same for everyone. Your loss affects you differently than anyone else.

If you are hurting right now, dealing with some kind of loss or tragedy, can I just say it is okay to still hurt. The old quote "Time heals all wounds" is not true! You may think about the person less often, or it may be less painful at times, but then the day comes when the pain cuts just as deep as the day the tragedy happened, and the scar is ripped open once again. Birthdays, holidays, the anniversary of their death, a song, a movie, a picture. So many things can trigger the hurt you felt that first day. The pain of loss doesn't just go away when the person isn't there anymore. It changes from the overwhelming, immense sadness of separation to wondering for the rest of your life about how different everything would be if they were still here. There is no timetable for grief. Don't carry that expectation for yourself, and certainly don't put it on someone else.

WHAT *CAN* YOU SAY OR DO?

Then what do you say to someone who is grieving? Honestly, there is no one right answer. There is no fix-all blanket statement that will ease the deep pain that accompanies the loss of a loved one.

Consider this: you don't have to say anything. Their grief is not for you to fix. There is no healing power in anything you can say.

Everyone deals with grief differently. What is helpful to one person may not be as helpful to another. A gift card to a coffee shop or restaurant is a gift someone can always use at the time they are ready to use it. However, taking someone out for coffee or a meal will allow them the chance to prepare for conversation when they are ready. A card of sympathy and love to show you care, a hug with no expectations for them to share anything, a simple *thinking about/praying for you and your family* or *I'm here for you* can speak volumes.

The truth about grief is that it is painful, messy, and unpredictable. While I may not always know the right things to say to a friend who is hurting, there is a Heavenly Father who loves them so much more than I ever could, and He knows what they need. Before saying the first thing that comes to your mind, pause and ask the Holy Spirit to give you the right words to say at the right time.

Just as the Father wrapped his loving arms around me and spoke words of kindness and healing, He desires to do that for you as well.

About the Author

I have no idea why in the world God would ask me to write a book.

I am not a writer.

I have never enjoyed writing.

I am not eloquent with words.

It was probably five years after our twins were born that John and I both felt the Lord wanted us to write a book. At that time, it just seemed right. Over the course of six more years the topic came up that we needed to start our book, or my father-in-law asked if we had started it yet, or a stranger after hearing just a small portion of Sarah's story would say to me, "You need to write a book." God has constantly reminded us of the task He has for us, but I just wasn't ready. I have constantly felt so inadequate for this undertaking. But I can't shake it. I can't escape it. I can't put it off any longer. A few years ago, God began preparing me. Preparing me for what exactly, I don't know. Something was changing.

I have never had the desire to do anything related to public speaking. The gripping stage fright that would take over any time I was in front of people was enough to send me crying and shaking after rehearsal. Yet, after a few years of singing backup on our church's worship team and having the opportunity to lead at times, the stage fright has become less gripping, and leading became more fulfilling.

One day in church I had an idea. If I was ever given the opportunity to preach, what would I want to say? I began a list of sermon ideas, which for someone who doesn't want to speak in front of people is a strange list to keep. This desire inside of me grew stronger, just waiting for someone to ask me to speak. The whole time, I'm thinking *what is wrong with me?!* I am not a teacher or preacher or leader in any way!

All my life I have been a listener. People confided, shared struggles, and told their stories to me. I listen and I listen well. But I've never felt like I really had anything good or helpful to say. Listening was my job, my gift. I didn't have enough Bible knowledge to share, or any tidbits of wisdom or a word of knowledge to impart, but I was willing to sit, to listen, and to cry. I am an empathetic person, so when you tell me about your pain, I feel it too. In 2017, we had taken a group of teenagers to youth camp as we did every summer. The leaders were having our morning meeting in the basement of the dining hall when I began praying for students. As

I stood in the back, the Holy Spirit surrounded me in such a powerful way that I couldn't help but just weep in His presence. He said to me, "You have something to say."

Sometimes I find myself arguing with God. Is it just me? Have you ever argued with God about what He is telling you to do? *Are you sure about that, God?*

Sometimes we think it's just our own thoughts that we are battling when it's the voice of God trying to lead us.

But then there are times, like this one, when I completely recognized His voice. It's when He speaks to me and all the fears and anxiety of the weight of the task seem to just melt away. It has taken me a while to finally realize that it doesn't matter that I didn't graduate from Bible college, or that I don't have as much scripture memorized as someone else, or that I wasn't as smart as this other person. God was telling me that I, too, have something to give to the students we are working with.

If my story can help just one person understand that they are not alone, it will all be worth it.

This desire to tell my story has continued to grow. If my story can help just one person understand that they are not alone, it will all be worth it. Bringing up the pain of the past has been extremely difficult, but while I know beyond a shadow of a doubt that God wants me to share my story with others, this process was also for me. I have realized there were lots of things that I hadn't dealt with yet. Pains I didn't want to talk about needed to be brought to the surface. I needed to take ownership of my wrong thinking, failures, and things I am ashamed to admit. One thing I've learned about pain and heartache is when brought into the open, healing can begin.

Appendix or Addendum

St. Louis Children's Hospital is part of the Barnes Jewish Hospital system. They produced a monthly newspaper in which we were asked if they could do a story on Sarah. It had been quite an ordeal for the hospital to send out two helicopters with two separate medical teams to transport our twins the day they were born.

Excerpt from the admission summary to Dr. Feth, Sarah's pediatrician.

PROBLEM LIST

1. Hyaline membrane disease status post surfactant administration. We will continue to follow her blood gases closely. We will adjust the ventilator as necessary. We will follow frequent exams and continuous pulse oximetry. We will maintain her oxygen saturations between 85 to 93%, pending

her clinical exam. We will consider early extubation to CPAP pending her clinical status.

2. GI/FEN: She will be initiated on total fluids of 80 mL/kg/day of D5W as well as starter TPN. She will be initiated on sodium acetate per umbilical arterial line to help maintain her acetate for the probable metabolic acidosis as we often see in prematurity. We will follow her urine as well as plasma electrolytes every six hours, adjust her fluids as necessary and follow her with daily weights and strict ins and outs. She will be n.p.o. at this time. Mother does desire to breastfeed.
3. Significant risk for hyperbilirubinemia secondary to prematurity, delayed enteral feeding and significant bruising. We will initiate phototherapy and follow her bilirubin on admission as well as every 12 hours.
4. Sepsis risk factors include prematurity and preterm labor. We will obtain blood cultures and a CBC, initiate ampicillin and gentamicin.
5. At risk for intraventricular hemorrhage. She will have a head ultrasound tomorrow.
6. At risk for anemia. We will follow her CBCs daily and transfuse as necessary.

7. At risk for retinopathy of prematurity. She will have an eye exam at approximately six weeks of age.
8. Thermodysregulation secondary to underlying prematurity. She will remain in an isolette.
9. At risk for apnea and bradycardia of prematurity. Should extubation be imminent, we will load her with caffeine. We will follow with continuous cardiorespiratory monitoring and pulse oximetry.
10. Thermodysregulation second to underlying prematurity: She is in a humidified Isolette.
11. At risk for apnea and bradycardia of prematurity: She will be loaded with caffeine in anticipation of early extubation.
12. Vascular access and blood sampling.

The plan was discussed with the primary care team. We will continue to follow twin A Jahnke for any life-threatening deterioration secondary to complications of her prematurity. We will follow with frequent exams, continuous pulse oximetry, continuous cardiorespiratory monitoring, and frequent labs.

OPERATIVE SUMMARY

07/01/2008

INDICATIONS FOR SURGERY: Sarah is a 2-week-old, ex-25 week estimated gestational age, infant with multiple problems of prematurity, including presumed infection, intraventricular hemorrhage, a GI bleed, and renal dysfunction. She also has what was felt to be a moderate sized patent ductus arteriosus which has been unresponsive to medical management. We have been asked to surgically ligate the ductus.

REFERRING PHYSICIAN LETTER

October 30, 2008

Dear Dr. Feth-Smith:

We had the pleasure of seeing your patient, Sarah Jahnke, in the Newborn Medicine follow-up clinic here at St. Louis Children's Hospital. Sarah is accompanied to the office today by her mother. As you may recall, Sarah is a former 25-4/7-week, 740 g, infant who was born to a 28-year-old, G1, P0, now 2 mother. She is now 4 months old, corrected age 1 month. Sarah's neonatal course was complicated by the following problems:

1. Chronic lung disease.
2. Grade III intraventricular hemorrhage with periventricular leukomalacia.
3. Hypothyroidism on Synthroid.
4. Retinopathy of prematurity, zone 2, stage 2, without plus disease bilaterally.
5. Left true vocal cord paralysis.
6. History of seizures now resolved.

7. Patent ductus arteriosus status post ligation.

8. Feeding intolerance with home NG feedings.

Sarah was discharged from the ICU on 10/01/2008. Since that time, she has done remarkably well. The family was able to remove her nasogastric tube approximately one week after discharge from the hospital. She since has been taking all of her feeds by mouth.

NEWS AND INFORMATION FOR THE PEOPLE WHO BRING BJC HEALTHCARE TO LIFE

BJC TODAY

AUGUST 4, 2008

INSIDE

da Vinci debuts at Boone
Surgeons introduce robotic system in July.

BJC's 'IronMoms' revealed
IronMom Foundation helps single moms reach their health, fitness goals.

Photo contest is on
Enter your photos in the 10th annual BJC TODAY employee photo contest.
PAGE 14

Beijing Bound
Nurse's son is on his way to the Olympics.
PAGE 24

HEADLINE NEWS
BJC PEOPLE
FOR YOUR BENEFITS
FOR YOUR HEALTH
VIEWPOINT
PAGE 14
WHERE YOU WORK
ETC.

BJC HealthCare

Saving baby Sarah

Children's Hospital offers last hope for surviving twin

Stephanie Jahnke holds her baby, Sarah, who is receiving care from nurses like Jennifer Jost, RN, in St. Louis Children's Hospital's newborn intensive care unit.

PAGES 12-13

Saving baby Sara

Children's Hospital

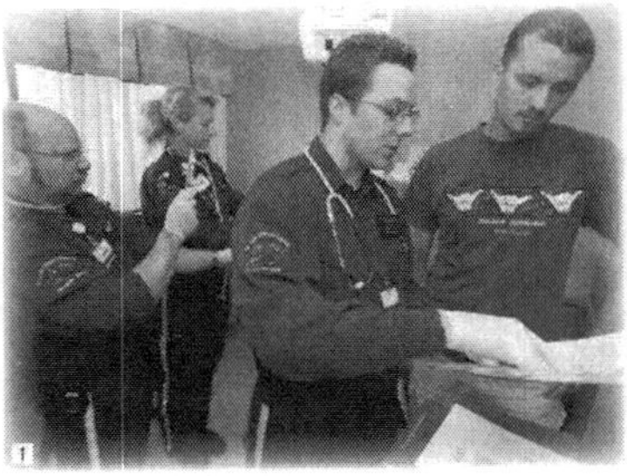

1

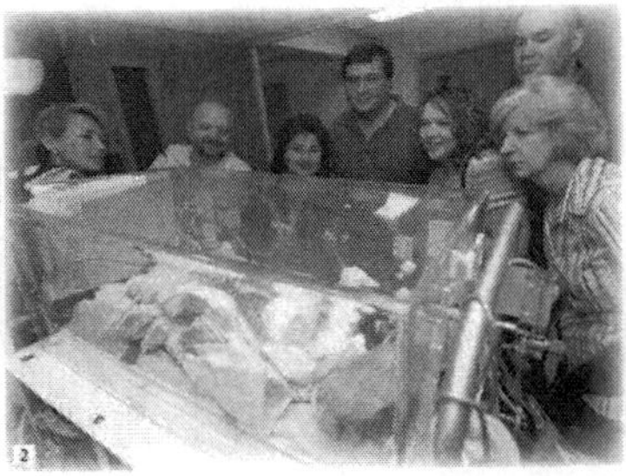

2

3

1. Tim Raney, EMT-P, far left, and Sabra Havey, RN, prepare the bed and medications for Sarah prior to delivery, while Dr. Jon Chiles reviews the care plan with John Jahnke, the babies' father.

2. Relatives of the parents watch as Sarah is wheeled out of the delivery room by Sabra Havey, RN, for the helicopter flight back to SLCH.

3. Sabra Havey, RN, draws a blood sample from Sarah during the return helicopter flight to SLCH.

4. Dr. Jon Chiles intubates Sarah after delivery before a breathing tube is placed.

5. Alanna receives care immediately after delivery. Born weighing just 1 pound, 14 ounces, she died three days later.

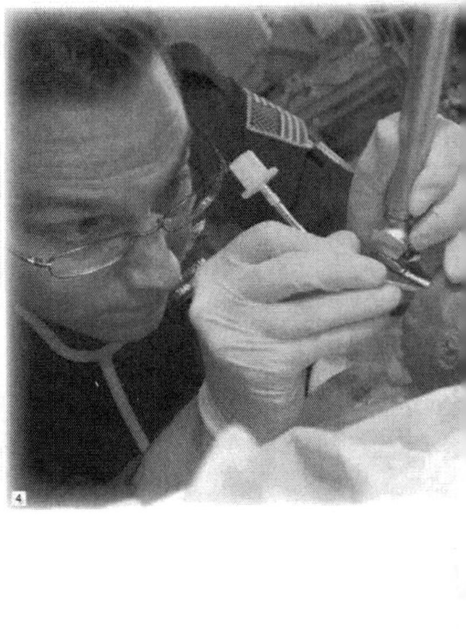

4

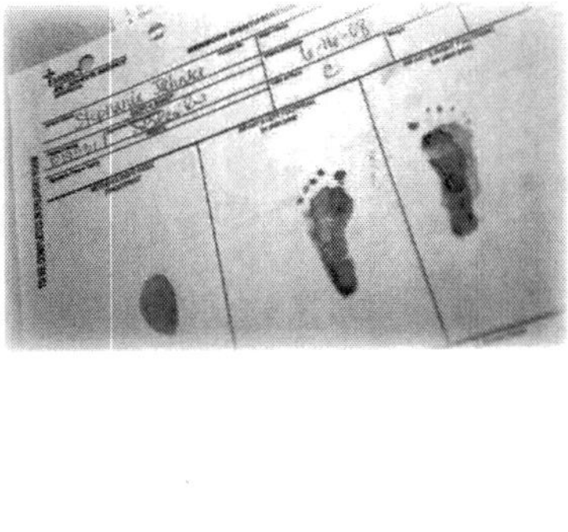

rs last hope for surviving twin

story and photos by John Twombly

It's June 16—the day after Father's Day—and John and Stephanie Jahnke clasp hands tightly as their delivery is about to begin at St. John's Mercy Hospital in Washington, Mo.

Sixty miles away, the St. Louis Children's Hospital transport team is dispatched in two helicopters to support the delivery, which occurs six months into the pregnancy due to pre-term labor. The transport team arrives at St. John's in about 20 minutes and within hours will bring the infants to SLCH. They will need highly specialized care available only at a major pediatric medical center — urgently.

First, Sarah is born, weighing just 1 pound, 10 ounces. Then it's Alanna, weighing 1 pound, 14 ounces. After the deliveries, the transport team administers care in the delivery room and then places each infant in an incubator for the return flight to SLCH.

Six weeks later, on July 30, Sarah is doing well in the newborn ICU—her weight has nearly doubled to 2 pounds, 12 ounces. Alanna, who was unable to overcome the multiple medical issues related to her premature birth, died June 19.

"The reality is that with premature babies, the outcome is uncertain," says Sabra Havey, RN, transport team. "The great outcomes are the reason why you do everything possible to save them—you just never know."

As for Sarah, her mother is grateful for her progress.

"Everyone at Children's Hospital has been good and helpful to us," Stephanie says. "I wouldn't want her anywhere else."

Editor's note: Although Alanna did not survive, her parents wanted her to be a part of this story, as she is a part of their lives.

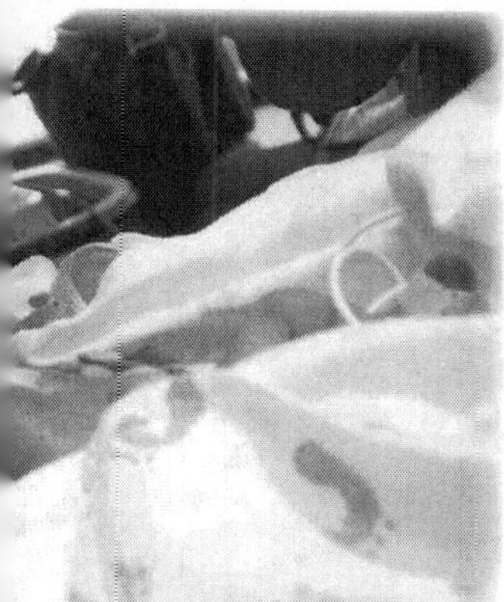

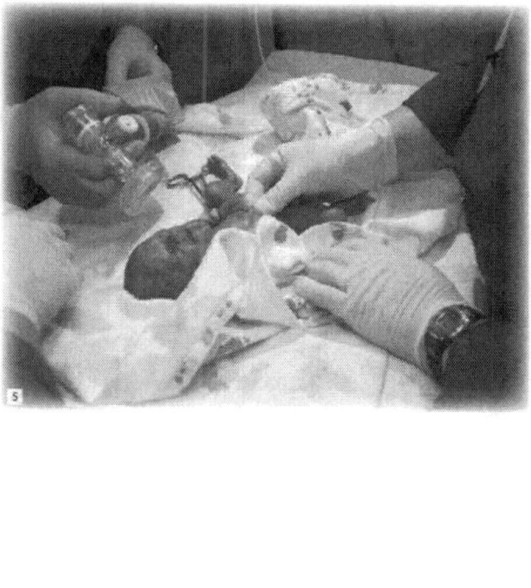

5

Endnotes

1. "Nothing Else" by Cody Carnes, Hank Bentley & Jessie Early, March 13, 2020

2. "Pivot on Your Good Foot - YouTube Videos" n.d. at 14:00-14:07 minutes

3. https://www.dictionary.com/browse/good

4. The Complete Biblical Library-The New Testament Greek-English Dictionary, Alpha-Gamma Word Numbers 1-1131. s.v. "18"